Grammar for Middle School

A Sentence-Composing Approach—
A Student Worktext

You'll never get anywhere with all those darn little short sentences.
—Gregory Clark, A *Social Perspective on the Function of Writing*

Grammar for Middle School

A Sentence-Composing Approach—
A Student Worktext

DON and JENNY KILLGALLON

HEINEMANN
Portsmouth, NH

Heinemann
361 Hanover Street
Portsmouth, NH 03801–3912
www.heinemann.com

Offices and agents throughout the world

© 2006 Don and Jenny Killgallon

All rights reserved. No part of this book may be reproduced in any form or by any electronic or mechanical means, including information storage and retrieval systems, without permission in writing from the publisher, except by a reviewer, who may quote brief passages in a review.

ISBN-13: 978-0-325-00956-8
ISBN-10: 0-325-00956-2

Editor: Lisa Luedeke
Production: Elizabeth Valway
Cover design: Shawn Girsberger
Typesetter: House of Equations, Inc.
Manufacturing: Jamie Carter

Printed in the United States of America on acid-free paper
18 EBM   13

To family and friends, for keeping the faith:
our thanks, our love.

Contents

Acknowledgments ix

IMITATING THE GRAMMAR OF THE GREATS 1
Activities to learn how to imitate the grammar of great writers. These first steps in sentence imitating will help you learn, practice, and use the fourteen sentence-composing tools in the rest of the worktext.

USING THE SENTENCE-COMPOSING TOOLBOX 10
A writing toolbox with fourteen sentence-composing tools to use to build better sentences. These tools are the kinds that professionals use for their sentences.

Words
Opening Adjective	12
Delayed Adjective	18
Opening Adverb	24
Delayed Adverb	30

Reviewing the Tools:
Michael Crichton's *Jurassic Park* 35

Phrases
Absolute Phrase	38
Appositive Phrase	44
Prepositional Phrase	50
Participial Phrase	56
Gerund Phrase	62
Infinitive Phrase	68

Reviewing the Tools:
J. R. R. Tolkien's *The Lord of the Rings* 73

Clauses
Clause Types (Independent, Dependent)	78
Adjective Clause	84
Adverb Clause	90
Noun Clause	96

Reviewing the Tools:
C. S. Lewis' *The Chronicles of Narnia* 101

CREATING GOOD WRITING 105
A review of the fourteen sentence-composing tools in the writing of J. K. Rowling, author of the Harry Potter novels. After reviewing the tools, you will use a variety of those tools to revise a paragraph and then to write an original episode for the Harry Potter story.

Acknowledgments

As you work through this worktext, you will learn grammatical tools of professional writers. As a result, you will create your own toolbox for composing sentences, develop your own writing style, and discover your own voice as a writer, while lastingly hearing the whispering of other voices—Michael Crichton's, J. R. R. Tolkien's, C. S. Lewis', J. K. Rowling's—and the hundreds of others on the following pages.

We thank all those writers whose model sentences transform literature into a legacy of lessons, providing for you voices of enduring value, voices that will help you discover your own.

Imitating the Grammar of the Greats

Why are the sentences of great authors more interesting, more memorable than the sentences of most people? One big reason is that their sentences are not monotonously built alike. Great authors and not-so-great writers use the same grammar—just in different ways. A huge difference is in the way those authors build their sentences. Authors build their sentences in lots of different ways. The purpose of this worktext is to learn those ways by acquiring the grammatical tools of authors and using those tools to build better sentences.

Look at the varied ways these sentences are built by J. K. Rowling, author of the Harry Potter novels:

1. He raised the wand above his head and brought it swishing down through the dusty air as a stream of red and gold sparks shot from the end like a firework, throwing dancing spots of light onto the walls.
   Harry Potter and the Sorcerer's Stone

2. Fifty years before, at daybreak on a fine summer's morning, when the Riddle House had still been well kept and impressive, a maid had entered the drawing room to find all three Riddles dead.
   Harry Potter and the Goblet of Fire

3. Harry paced the bedroom waiting for Hedwig to come back, his head pounding, his brain too busy for sleep even though his eyes stung and itched with tiredness.
   Harry Potter and the Order of the Phoenix

In the pages of this worktext, you will analyze, study, and then imitate the sentences of J. K. Rowling and many other authors of books often read by students in the middle grades—including Michael Crichton (*Jurassic Park*), J. R. R. Tolkien (*The Lord of the Rings*), C. S. Lewis (*The Chronicles of Narnia*)—to learn and practice and use in your writing fourteen grammatical tools for building your own sentences in better ways. With the many practices in *Grammar for Middle School: A Sentence-Composing Approach*, you can create your own personal toolbox of sentence-composing tools.

And guess what? By the end of the worktext, if you learn the fourteen magical tools covered, you will be able to write sentences built just like ones by J. K. Rowling! How? The secret is learning to imitate the grammatical tools of authors for building good sentences. In the following pages, you'll learn how.

Okay, let's get started on your way to building better—*much better*—sentences. All you need to succeed is your determination to learn to build sentences the way authors like Michael Crichton, J. R. R. Tolkien, C. S. Lewis, and J. K. Rowling build theirs.

Imitating the Grammar of the Greats

Chunking to Imitate

In these exercises you will become aware of meaningful divisions within sentences, an awareness you'll need to imitate model sentences. You will learn that authors compose their sentences one "chunk" or meaningful sentence part at a time.

Directions (Part One): From each pair of sentences below, select the sentence that is divided into meaningful chunks and copy it on your paper.

1a. He was still there / in front of the window, / staring at the saddle, / when two cowhands / came out / of the nearest saloon.

1b. He was / still there in front of / the window, staring at / the saddle, when two / cowhands came out of the / nearest saloon.
Hal Borland, *When the Legends Die*

2a. Then she turned away / from my curious stare / and left the room, / crying.

2b. Then she turned / away from my curious / stare and left the / room, crying.
Christy Brown, *My Left Foot*

3a. Shiloh's under the / sycamore, head on his paws, just / like the day he followed me home.

3b. Shiloh's under the sycamore, / head on his paws, / just like the day he followed me home.
Phyllis Reynolds Naylor, *Shiloh*

Directions (Part Two): Copy each model sentence below and then copy the sentence that can be divided into chunks that match the chunks in the model.

1. MODEL: I decided / not to open my eyes, / not to get out of bed.
Rosa Guy, *The Friends*

   a. Running to catch the bus, I fell and dropped my books.
   b. I wanted only to get the best grade, only to be the best in the class.

2. MODEL: Soon a glow began / in the dark, / a tiny circle barely red.
Joseph Krumgold, *Onion John*

Imitating the Grammar of the Greats

   a. Then a sound came through the night, a small rustle hardly heard.
   b. We planned carefully for the party, wanting it to be a success.

3. MODEL: Finally, / I sit on a log, / put my gun at my feet, / and wait.
   Phyllis Reynolds Naylor, *Shiloh*

   a. Wondering what to do next, I just lean against the wall and stare into the sky.
   b. Occasionally, I walk down the path, carry my camera around my neck, and look.

Directions (Part Three): Copy the model and then copy the sentence that imitates it. Then chunk both the model and the sentence that imitates it into meaningful sentence parts, using a slash mark (/).

1. MODEL: His face was bloody, his shirt torn and bloody down the front.
   Hal Borland, *When the Legends Die*

   a. The day was perfect, the sky blue and perfect in the heavens.
   b. His sister married someone they didn't know, a stranger to the family.

2. MODEL: Big, rough teenagers jostled through the crowd, their sleeves rolled high enough to show off blue and red tattoos.
   Robert Lipsyte, *The Contender*

   a. An old, large man reached for the available chair and sat down, huffing and puffing, before I could get there.
   b. Silent, silver fish moved through the tank, their bodies sleek enough to suggest larger and more dangerous predators.

Directions (Part Four): Match the model with the sentence that most closely imitates it. Copy both sentences. Then chunk both, using a slash (/) between sentence parts. Finally, write your own imitation of each model.

1. MODEL: Then, stomach down on the bed, he began to draw.
   Katherine Paterson, *Bridge to Terabithia*

2. MODEL: Slowly, filled with dissatisfaction, he had gone to his room and got into bed.
   Betsy Byars, *The Summer of the Swans*

Imitating the Grammar of the Greats

IMITATIONS

a. Carefully, embarrassed by her mistake, she had repeated the process and done it correctly.

b. Later, knapsack high on his back, he ran to catch up.

Imitating the Grammar of the Greats

Unscrambling to Imitate

The unscrambling of sentence parts helps you see how those parts are connected within the model sentence. As a result, you will glimpse the mind of an author composing a sentence so you can go through a similar process when you compose sentences.

Directions: Unscramble the sentence parts to imitate the model. Then write your own sentence that imitates the model.

1. MODEL: When I awoke, there were snowflakes on my eyes.
   Charles Portis, *True Grit*

   a. in the sky
   b. there was a rainbow
   c. after the rain stopped

2. MODEL: Drawn by the scent of fish, the wild dogs sat on the hill, barking and growling at each other.
   Scott O'Dell, *Island of the Blue Dolphins*

   a. yelping and trembling with delight
   b. covered with mud from the yard
   c. the frisky puppy rolled on the carpet

3. MODEL: Then she swung the switch five more times and, discovering Little Man had no intention of crying, ordered him up.
   Mildred D. Taylor, *Roll of Thunder, Hear My Cry*

   a. one more time and
   b. walked away
   c. then he checked the crime scene
   d. finding the suspect had been telling the truth

4. MODEL: The girls of her class nearly fought to hang out around her, to walk away with her, to beam flatteringly, to be her special friend.
   Katherine Mansfield, *The Doll House*

Imitating the Grammar of the Greats

a. really tried to make his best effort with the team
b. to keep up with the them
c. to be his absolute best
d. the boy of smallest size
e. to work tirelessly

Imitating the Grammar of the Greats

Combining to Imitate

These exercises ask you to combine a series of plain sentences into just one varied sentence by changing the plain sentences into sentence parts resembling the model sentence. As you do these exercises, you'll become aware that plain sentences can easily be changed into sentence parts of better, more varied sentences.

Directions: Combine the sentences below to create a single sentence that has the same order of sentence parts as the model. You may eliminate some words to do so. Then write your own imitation of the model.

1. MODEL: The children, shouting and screaming, came charging back into their homeroom.
   Rosa Guy, The Friends

   a. The ponies were neighing.
   b. The ponies were pawing.
   c. The ponies came bolting out of their stalls.

2. MODEL: As Seabiscuit broke from the gate, he was immediately bashed inward by Count Atlas, a hopeless long shot emerging from the stall on Seabiscuit's right.
   Laura Hillenbrand, Seabiscuit: An American Legend

   a. Something happened as the car backed out of the space.
   b. What happened was that it was suddenly hit sideways.
   c. The hit was by an oncoming truck.
   d. The truck was a delivery pickup.
   e. The pickup was coming from the alley behind the market.

3. MODEL: A light kindled in the sky, a blaze of yellow fire behind dark barriers.
   J. R. R. Tolkien, The Lord of the Rings

   a. A noise erupted.
   b. The noise erupted from the forest.
   c. The noise was a screech.
   d. The screech was of angry ravens.
   e. The ravens were in decaying trees.

Imitating the Grammar of the Greats

4. MODEL: He knew the bears would soon be leaving their winter dens, to travel, to claim their old ranges, to challenge intruders, and to fight their fearful battles among themselves.

     Hal Borland, *When the Legends Die*

   a. She knew something about the students.
   b. She knew they would soon be entering their new classrooms.
   c. The students would be entering the classrooms to learn.
   d. They would also be entering them to take new courses.
   e. They would also be entering them to make new friends.
   f. And they would be entering them to discover their identities as young adults.

Imitating the Grammar of the Greats

Imitating Alone

Once you have learned how to imitate professional sentences, you will be able to easily imitate almost any professional sentence just by seeing how the model is built and then building your own sentence in a similar way.

Directions: Choose one of the models and write an imitation of the entire sentence, one sentence part at a time. See if your classmates can guess your model.

Models:

1. He was white and shaking, / his mouth opening and shutting / without words.
   Leslie Morris, "Three Shots for Charlie Beston"

2. Now, / leaning his head out of the window / of the pickup, / he thought he would die of thirst.
   Katherine Paterson, *Park's Quest*

3. Hobbling on one foot, / Wanda opened the closet door / and turned on the light.
   Betsy Byars, *The Summer of the Swans*

4. Propped on her elbows / with her chin in her fists, / she stared at the black wolf, / trying to catch his eye.
   Jean Craighead George, *Julie of the Wolves*

Using the Sentence-Composing Toolbox

The sentence-composing toolbox on the following pages is the heart of this worktext. It provides instruction in and varied practices with tools that professional writers use in their sentences so that you can learn to use those tools within your own writing. No tool is more difficult than the others. Although some may be new to you, all of them are easy to learn.

Format for Each of the Tools

Definition—A concise, clear grammatical description of the tool, often presented with tips to identify the tool.

Examples—Professional sentences containing the tool in **bold type**.

Sentence Bank—A list of six model sentences: three with a single example of the tool, three with multiple examples.

Varied Practices—After an introductory matching exercise, the sentence-composing techniques—unscrambling, combining, imitating, expanding—vary the ways in which the tool is practiced.

Creative Writing—Designed to improve paragraphs through building better sentences, this activity applies the new tool and others you've already learned within your own writing, without imitating. Previous practices in imitating will help because you can use tools like the ones in the professional models you imitated.

Imitating Sentences of the Pros

In the following practices, through imitating professional sentences you'll build your sentences to resemble sentences of published authors, using the "grammar of the greats."

Prewriting
As you plan your sentences, jot down several ideas for interesting content, maybe something from a book, movie, TV show, current or historical event, or a topic from a piece of writing you are working on in school.

Rewriting
Another possibility is to revise something you've already written for any class or something you wrote on your own. To revise, compose a sentence imitation to include in that piece.

Using the Sentence-Composing Toolbox

Becoming a Pro
When you decide what to write about, consider yourself a professional author, a pro! Through several revisions, make the content as "professional" as the structure you're imitating. Compose a memorable sentence to share with your classmates!

Using the Sentence-Composing Toolbox

Sentence-Composing Tools: Opening Adjective

DEFINITION

An adjective at the opening of a sentence. The adjective may be a single adjective or the first word in an adjective phrase. A comma follows an opening adjective.

Single adjective: **Comfortable**, I lay on my back and waited for sleep, and while waiting I thought of Dill.
Harper Lee, *To Kill a Mockingbird*

Adjective phrase: **Able to move now**, he rocked his own body back and forth, breathing deeply to release the remembered pain.
Lois Lowry, *The Giver*

Single Opening Adjectives:

1. **Rigid**, I began climbing the rungs, slightly reassured by having Finny right behind me.
John Knowles, *A Separate Peace*

2. **Hungry**, Thomas ate two portions of meat, nothing else.
Hal Borland, *When the Legends Die*

3. **Always meticulously neat**, six-year-old Little Man never allowed dirt or tears or stains to mar anything he owned.
Mildred D. Taylor, *Roll of Thunder, Hear My Cry*

Multiple Opening Adjectives:

4. **Slow** and **lumbering**, he looked as if he had slept in his clothes, and in fact he often did, after a marathon programming session.
Michael Crichton, *Prey*

5. **Rain-drenched, fresh, vital, full of life**, spring enveloped all of us.
Mildred D. Taylor, *Roll of Thunder, Hear My Cry*

Using the Sentence-Composing Toolbox

6. **Certain of herself, certain of her friends in the house, certain of her voice and her success,** Carlotta flung herself into her part without restraint of modesty.

    Gaston Leroux, *The Phantom of the Opera*

PRACTICE 1: MATCHING

Match the opening adjectives at the caret (^) with the sentences. Write out each sentence, inserting and underlining them.

Sentences:

1. ^ the boy leaped forward and grabbed the ball from Charles Wallace's hand, then darted back into the shadows.

    Madeleine L'Engle, *A Wrinkle in Time*

2. ^ he was seated upon a throne which was at the same time both simple and majestic.

    Antoine de Saint-Exupéry, *The Little Prince*

3. ^ Romey folded his hands in his lap and closed his eyes.

    Bill and Vera Cleaver, *Where the Lilies Bloom*

4. ^ they sloshed through the cavernous sewer.

    Sid Fleischman, *The Whipping Boy*

5. ^ the rabbit paddled and struggled, got his head up and took a breath, scrabbled his claws against rough bricks under water and lost them again as he was dragged on.

    Richard Adams, *Watership Down*

Opening Adjectives:

a. Prissy like a girl,

b. Clad in royal purple and ermine,

c. Deeper and deeper, darker and darker,

d. Quick as a flash,

e. Full of fear,

Using the Sentence-Composing Toolbox

PRACTICE 2: UNSCRAMBLING TO IMITATE

In the model and the scrambled list, identify the opening adjective. Next, unscramble and write out the sentence parts to imitate the model. Finally, write your own imitation of the model and identify the opening adjective.

MODEL: Desperate, Frodo drew his own sword, and it seemed to him that it flickered red, as if it were a firebrand.

J. R. R. Tolkien, *The Lord of the Rings*

a. that the board shook violently

b. and it appeared to him

c. as if it were a trampoline

d. nervous

e. Jackson walked the diving board

PRACTICE 3: COMBINING TO IMITATE

In the model, identify the opening adjective. Next, combine the list of sentences to imitate the model (you may omit some words). Finally, write your own imitation of the model and identify the opening adjective.

MODEL: Curious, Captain Cook started walking round and round the tripod, until the clothesline, the penguin, Mr. Popper and the tripod were all tangled up.

Richard and Florence Atwater, *Mr. Popper's Penguins*

a. Lewis was late.

b. Lewis began running faster and faster to homeroom class.

c. This continued until something happened.

d. What happened was that the vice principal, the hall duty teacher, and his homeroom teacher were all summoned there.

Using the Sentence-Composing Toolbox

PRACTICE 4: IMITATING

Identify the opening adjectives in the models and sample imitations. Then choose one of the models and write an imitation of the entire sentence, one sentence part at a time. See if your classmates can guess your model.

Models:

1. Cheerful and exuberant, he was the kind of fellow to slap a man on the back with a greeting.

    Oscar Hijuelos, *The Fourteen Sisters of Emilio Montez O'Brien*

    Sample: Lighthearted and optimistic, she was the sort of child to spread sunshine in a gathering through her smile.

2. Numb of all feeling, empty as a shell, still he clung to life, and the hours droned by.

    Armstrong Sperry, *Call It Courage*

    Sample: Full of vivid colors, vibrant as a rainbow, soon the garden burst into bloom, and the visitors lined up.

3. Arrestingly handsome, George had dark blonde hair that cruised back from a part he kept just a nudge off center, as was the fashion.

    Laura Hillenbrand, *Seabiscuit: An American Legend*

    Sample: Disturbingly quiet, Sarah had large somber eyes that looked out from a face she left unadorned every day, as was her habit.

PRACTICE 5: EXPANDING

Below are sentences with the opening adjectives omitted at the caret mark (^). For each caret, add an opening adjective (word or phrase), blending your content and style with the rest of the sentence.

1. ^, now soaked all down her front, Tisha pushed onward.

    Stephen King, *The Girl Who Loved Tom Gordon*

Using the Sentence-Composing Toolbox

2. ^, Roger sought a way out.

   Tom Wolfe, *A Man in Full*

3. ^, they jumped first on Teft.

   Glendon Swarthout, *Bless the Beasts and the Children*

CREATIVE WRITING

Composing a paragraph—Pretend that you are one of the professional writers listed below who has written the first sentence of a long story. Use one of the sentences as the first sentence in a paragraph that will begin that story. Create the rest of the paragraph. Just as the writers' sentences use opening adjectives, within your paragraph use opening adjectives and other sentence-composing tools you've learned to make your paragraph memorable.

Reminder: Don't try to write a complete story. Write only the first paragraph of that story. (Maybe later you'll want to write the entire story!)

1. **Rigid with fear**, sitting up in bed, I stared helplessly as a face rose up in the moonlit window.

   R. L. Stine, *Ghost Beach*

2. **Deep in the forest**, there was a green lawn, and on the lawn stood a miserable little hut on hen's legs, where lived Baba-Yaga, an old witch grandmother.

   Post Wheeler, *Vasilissa the Beautiful*

3. **Full of fear**, the rabbit paddled and struggled, got his head up and took a breath, scrabbled his claws against rough bricks under water and lost them again as he was dragged on.

   Richard Adams, *Watership Down*

Using the Sentence-Composing Toolbox

Sentence-Composing Tools: Delayed Adjective

DEFINITION

An adjective placed after the word described. The adjective may be a single adjective or the first word in an adjective phrase. Commas punctuate and separate the delayed adjectives or adjective phrases from the other parts of the sentence: one comma if the delayed adjective ends the sentence, two if it occurs earlier.

Single adjective: He paused in his humming song, and the bear's ears stiffened, **alert**.
          Hal Borland, *When the Legends Die*

Adjective phrase: Gwydion sat upright, **tense as a bowstring**.
          Lloyd Alexander, *The Book of Three*

I stared at the trees, **aware of an eerie silence descending over the forest**.
          Mildred D. Taylor, *Song of the Trees*

Single Delayed Adjectives:

1. A woman of fifty or so, **plump with frizzy gray hair**, came toward them.
          Katherine Paterson, *Park's Quest*

2. A circle of grass, **smooth as a lawn**, met her eyes, with dark trees dancing all round it.
          C. S. Lewis, *The Chronicles of Narnia*

3. Jonas felt more and more certain that the destination lay ahead of him, **very near now in the night that was approaching**.
          Lois Lowry, *The Giver*

Multiple Delayed Adjectives:

4. The Indian lay there on the floor of the cupboard, **stiff** and **stark**.
          Lynne Reid Banks, *The Indian in the Cupboard*

5. A voice suddenly shouted at me, **loud** and **strong** and **angry**, although I couldn't understand the words.
          Robert Cormier, *Take Me Where the Good Times Are*

Using the Sentence-Composing Toolbox

6. The first thing Rainsford's eyes discerned was the largest man Rainsford had ever seen, a gigantic creature, **solidly made** and **black-bearded to the waist**.

    Richard Connell, *The Most Dangerous Game*

PRACTICE 1: MATCHING

Match the delayed adjectives with the sentences. Write out each sentence, inserting the delayed adjectives at the caret (^) and underlining them.

Sentences:

1. Her eyes glared, ^, from beneath arched black wings of brows.
    Lois Duncan, *A Gift of Magic*

2. Sitting beside the tree, Millie opened her packages slowly, ^.
    Jean Fritz, *Homesick: My Own Story*

3. Harry looked at his mother, who had her back to him, ^.
    Norman Katkov, "The Torn Invitation"

4. He surveyed the roof carefully, ^, indicating the places where it would have to be repaired.
    William E. Barrett, *The Lilies of the Field*

5. He ate while his blanket, ^, steamed in front of the fire.
    Hal Borland, *When the Legends Die*

Delayed Adjectives:

a. still damp

b. sharp and bright

c. aware from the markings that someone had surveyed it before him

d. busy at the stove

e. careful to untie the ribbons, careful not to tear the paper

PRACTICE 2: UNSCRAMBLING TO IMITATE

In the model and the scrambled list, identify the delayed adjectives. Next, unscramble and write out the sentence parts to imitate the model. Finally, write your own imitation of the model and identify the delayed adjectives.

Using the Sentence-Composing Toolbox

MODEL: The swift-flowing clouds lifted and melted away, and the sun came out, pale and bright.

J. R. R. Tolkien, *The Lord of the Rings*

a. opened and filled fast

b. and the new Jaguar

c. sleek and shiny

d. the long-awaited car show

e. stood out

PRACTICE 3: COMBINING TO IMITATE

In the model, identify the delayed adjectives. Next, combine the list of sentences to imitate the model. Finally, write your own imitation of the model and identify the delayed adjectives.

MODEL: She sat there, very still and white and thoughtful.

Roald Dahl, *Matilda*

a. The cat jumped up.

b. The cat was very silent.

c. And the cat was black.

d. And the cat was creepy.

PRACTICE 4: IMITATING

Identify the delayed adjectives in the models and sample imitations. Then choose one of the models and write an imitation of the entire sentence, one sentence part at a time. See if your classmates can guess your model.

Models:

1. Through her tears she could see Charles Wallace standing there, very small, very white.

Madeleine L'Engle, *A Wrinkle in Time*

Sample: Near the door he could hear the puppy whimpering outside, very softly, very sadly.

Using the Sentence-Composing Toolbox

2. The door swung wide then, and an elderly woman, frail and toothless, stepped out.
   Mildred D. Taylor, *Roll of Thunder, Hear My Cry*

   Sample: The bus pulled up outside, and a small child, confident and independent, got off.

3. Jemmy gorged himself, anxious to be off and not certain when he would eat again.
   Sid Fleischman, *The Whipping Boy*

   Sample: Shea admired herself, careful to check everything and absolutely sure that she could look no better.

PRACTICE 5: EXPANDING

Below are sentences with the delayed adjectives omitted at the caret mark (^). For each caret, add a delayed adjective (word or phrase), blending your content and style with the rest of the sentence.

1. The raft continued on, and they smelled a peculiar odor, ^.
   Michael Crichton, *Jurassic Park*

2. At one point a raven, ^, came flapping out from a bush and flew alongside us, his hoarse "tok, tok" weird and hollow.
   Bill and Vera Cleaver, *Where the Lilies Bloom*

3. Laughter, ^, filled the room.
   Rosa Guy, *The Friends*

CREATIVE WRITING

Revising a paragraph—To revise the plain paragraph below, at the caret marks (^) add delayed adjectives or other sentence-composing tools you've already learned.

"The Oldest Toy"

1. Rachel stared at her ruined doll, ^.
2. ^, she had played with that toy every day.
3. Her parents had given her other toys, ^, but she always loved this doll the most.
4. ^, she looked down at the broken doll, ^.

Using the Sentence-Composing Toolbox

5. ^, the doll lay there, and, ^, she wiped her tears away, ^.

6. Rachel knew that birthdays would bring her more presents, ^, and new toys to play with, ^, but none could replace her doll.

Write out your revision like a paragraph, not a list of sentences. Present your revised paragraph to your class to see the various effective ways you and your classmates revised the same plain paragraph to make it memorable.

Tip for Better Revising: Always, when you revise something you've written, look for places to use delayed adjectives and other sentence-composing tools to add detail, interest, and professional style to your writing.

Using the Sentence-Composing Toolbox

Sentence Composing Tools: Opening Adverb

DEFINITION

An adverb at the beginning of a sentence. A comma follows an opening adverb. All adverbs give information about an action.

Adverbs that tell how an action happened (*quickly, slowly, rapidly*) almost always end in *ly*. Other adverbs tell *when* an action happened (*now, then, yesterday*), or *where* an action happened (*overhead, nearby, underneath*).

How: **Quickly**, they flung a rope with a hook towards him.
J. R. R. Tolkien, *The Hobbit*

When: **Overnight**, Jem had acquired an alien set of values and was trying to impose them on me.
Harper Lee, *To Kill a Mockingbird*

Where: **Outside**, beyond the low, white fence, a wagonette with a pair of cabs was waiting.
Sir Arthur Conan Doyle, *The Hound of the Baskervilles*

Single Opening Adverbs:

1. **Reluctantly**, the boy fastened the collar on the bear cub.
   Hal Borland, *When the Legends Die*

2. **Soon**, he reached the thicket of pepper trees.
   Carl Hiassen, *Hoot*

3. **Slyly**, I tried to check my teammates for any sign that they recognized the wrongness of the movement.
   Pat Conroy, *My Losing Season*

Multiple Opening Adverbs:

4. **Quickly** and **quietly**, over the guard's head, George walked away.
   Hans Augusto Rey, *Curious George*

5. **On** and **on**, they walked, but the view did not vary.
   J. K. Rowling, *Harry Potter and the Half-Blood Prince*

Using the Sentence-Composing Toolbox

6. **Instantly, obediently**, Jonas had dropped his bike on its side on the path behind his family's dwelling.

    Lois Lowry, *The Giver*

PRACTICE 1: MATCHING

Match the opening adverbs with the sentences. Write out each sentence, inserting the opening adverbs at the caret (^) and underlining them.

Sentences:

1. ^ the branches rustled.
    Lloyd Alexander, *The Book of Three*

2. ^ I climbed over the scraggly rocks, slippery from the evening dew.
    R. L. Stine, *Ghost Beach*

3. ^ like a mother with a little child, she led the heartbroken old man out of the watchers' line of vision, out of the circle of lamplight.
    F. R. Buckley, "Gold-Mounted Guns"

4. ^ the snake raised its head until its eyes were on a level with Harry's.
    J. K. Rowling, *Harry Potter and the Sorcerer's Stone*

5. ^ she limped across the room and sat in her chair by the window.
    Eleanor Coerr, *Sadako and the Thousand Paper Cranes*

Opening Adverbs:

a. Gently,

b. Overhead,

c. Slowly, very slowly,

d. Unsteadily,

e. Up, up,

PRACTICE 2: UNSCRAMBLING TO IMITATE

In the model and the scrambled list, identify the opening adverb. Next, unscramble and write out the sentence parts to imitate the model. Finally, write your own imitation of the model and identify the opening adverb.

Using the Sentence-Composing Toolbox

MODEL: Slowly, she slid the rest of the way down, and vanished.

Michael Crichton, *Prey*

a. she washed the grease from the plate

b. carefully

c. and rinsed

PRACTICE 3: COMBINING TO IMITATE

In the model, identify the opening adverbs. Next, combine the list of sentences to imitate the model. Finally, write your own imitation of the model and identify the opening adverbs.

MODEL: Up, up, Icarus went, soaring into the bright sun.

Olivia Coolidge, *Daedalus*

a. Around, around, Rex chased.

b. He was circling around his own tail.

PRACTICE 4: IMITATING

Identify the opening adverbs in the models and sample imitations. Then choose one of the models and write an imitation of the entire sentence, one sentence part at a time. See if your classmates can guess your model.

Models:

1. Twice, when the train lurched, he sat up, looking around fiercely.

   Robert Lipsyte, *The Contender*

   Sample: Sometimes, when the sun dazzled, she went outside, playing outdoors joyfully.

2. Later, when it was time for the smaller children in the cabin to go to bed, Sounder's master got up, put on his overall jacket, and went outside.

   William Armstrong, *Sounder*

Using the Sentence-Composing Toolbox

Sample: Sometimes, after it had been repeatedly announced for students to put their books away, the teacher walked forward, picked up the chalk, and wrote down names.

3. Further south, they saw the graceful necks of the apatosaurs, standing at the water's edge, their bodies mirrored in the moving surface.

    Michael Crichton, *Jurassic Park*

Sample: Once daily, Jenny picked an armful of lovely flowers, strolling throughout the garden, her smile lit by the sun.

PRACTICE 5: EXPANDING

Below are sentences with the opening adverbs omitted at the caret mark (^). For each caret, add an opening adverb, blending your content and style with the rest of the sentence.

1. ^, Jonas concentrated on the screen, waiting for what would happen next.

    Lois Lowry, *The Giver*

2. ^ and ^, they drove through the darkness, and though the rain stopped, the wind rushed by and whistled and made strange sounds.

    Frances Hodgson Burnett, *The Secret Garden*

3. ^, ^ and ^, he got up.

    Lynne Reid Banks, *The Indian in the Cupboard*

CREATIVE WRITING

Composing a paragraph—Pretend that you are one of the professional writers listed below who has written the first sentence of a long story. Use one of the sentences as the first sentence in a paragraph that will begin that story. Create the rest of the paragraph. Just as the writers' sentences use opening adverbs, within your paragraph use opening adverbs and other sentence-composing tools you've learned to make your paragraph memorable.

Reminder: Don't try to write a complete story. Write only the first paragraph of that story! (Maybe later you'll want to write the entire story!)

Using the Sentence-Composing Toolbox

1. **Outside**, she saw only a calm, beautiful night.
   Walter Lord, *A Night to Remember*

2. **Suddenly**, coming out of Turn 5 on the fifth lap, the race again became a contest instead of a Sunday drive.
   Gene Olson, *The Roaring Road*

3. **Then**, as quickly as it had become a tiger, the specter changed into a man with the face of a rat.
   Walter Dean Myers, *Legend of Tarik*

Using the Sentence-Composing Toolbox

Sentence-Composing Tools: Delayed Adverb

DEFINITION

An adverb placed after and away from the action described. All adverbs give information about an action.

Adverbs that tell how an action happened (*quickly, slowly, rapidly*) almost always end in *ly*. Other adverbs tell *when* an action happened (*now, then, yesterday*), or *where* an action happened (*overhead, nearby, underneath*).

How: The hand of the dinosaur pushed aside the ferns, **slowly**.
Michael Crichton, Jurassic Park

When: When I was safe in bed, I'd peek, **sometimes**.
Mercer Mayer, There's a Nightmare in My Closet

Where: Their path wound, **in** and **out**, through the scrub, around palmetto clumps, over trunks of fallen trees, under dwarf pines and oaks.
Lois Lenski, Strawberry Girl

Single Delayed Adverbs:

1. The three clouds rose up together, **smoothly**.
Michael Crichton, Prey

2. For a long time, Muley looked at him, **timidly**.
John Steinbeck, The Grapes of Wrath

3. Jem opened the gate, **slowly** as possible, lifting it aside and resting it on the fence.
Harper Lee, To Kill a Mockingbird

Multiple Delayed Adverbs:

4. After ten minutes or so we got back in the car and drove out to the main road, **slowly** and **carefully**.
Stephen King, Everything's Eventual

Using the Sentence-Composing Toolbox

5. The gigantic snake was nearing Frank, and then, **incredibly, miraculously**, it passed him, following the spitting, hissing noises made by the cold voice beyond the door.
    J. K. Rowling, *Harry Potter and the Goblet of Fire*

6. If Sam had looked back, he might have seen not far below Gollum turn again, and then with a wild light of madness glaring in his eyes come, **swiftly** but **warily**, creeping on behind, a slinking shadow among the stones.
    J. R. R. Tolkien, *The Lord of the Rings*

PRACTICE 1: MATCHING

Match the delayed adverbs with the sentences. Write out each sentence, inserting the delayed adverbs at the caret (^) and underlining them.

Sentences:

1. In the fishpond, the hippo belched, ^.
    Hugo Leon, "My Father and the Hippopotamus"

2. She watched the children troop in, ^, an ancient nursery rhyme running through her head.
    Mary Elizabeth Vroman, "See How They Run"

3. His body glided quietly across the room, ^.
    John Steinbeck, *The Pearl*

4. Someone was humming under her breath, ^.
    Ray Bradbury, *The Martian Chronicles*

5. Jonas, ^, remembered the time in his childhood when he had been chastised for misusing a word.
    Lois Lowry, *The Giver*

Delayed Adverbs:

a. high and sweetly

b. noiselessly and smoothly

c. not softly

d. suddenly and grimly

e. very noisily

Using the Sentence-Composing Toolbox

PRACTICE 2: UNSCRAMBLING TO IMITATE

In the model and the scrambled list, identify the delayed adverb. Next, unscramble and write out the sentence parts to imitate the model. Finally, write your own imitation of the model and identify the delayed adverb.

MODEL: Alfred moved on, quickly, angry at the sudden sting in his eyes, and the sudden emptiness in his stomach.
>Robert Lipsyte, *The Contender*

a. cautiously

b. and her status with the class

c. the new student walked in

d. uncertain about her admission to the school

PRACTICE 3: COMBINING TO IMITATE

In the model, identify the delayed adverb. Next, combine the list of sentences to imitate the model. Finally, write your own imitation of the model and identify the delayed adverb.

MODEL: When the bell rang for recess, he put on his red jacket and walked alone, outside.
>Louis Sachar, *There's a Boy in the Girl's Bathroom*

a. This happened after his mother called her son for dinner.

b. What happened was Patrick put away his bicycle.

c. And Patrick came inside.

d. He came inside eagerly.

PRACTICE 4: IMITATING

Identify the delayed adverbs in the models and sample imitations. Then choose one of the models and write an imitation of the entire sentence, one sentence part at a time. See if your classmates can guess your model.

Using the Sentence-Composing Toolbox

Models:

1. He barked once, severely.
   Stephen King, Needful Things

   Sample: He turned away, guiltily.

2. He spoke on, firmly and clearly, with such joyful enthusiasm that Eilonwy had no heart to stop him.
   Lloyd Alexander, The High King

   Sample: Sammy edged forward, slowly and reluctantly, with such awful dread that his dad had no desire to encourage him.

3. Griffin was light and fast, his gloves a red blur tapping away at Alfred's face, easily and steadily as rain on a roof.
   Robert Lipsyte, The Contender

   Sample: The painting was striking and quirky, its colors a kaleidoscope bursting off of the canvas, raucously and dramatically as art in your face.

PRACTICE 5: EXPANDING

Below are sentences with the delayed adverbs omitted at the caret mark (^). For each caret, add a delayed adverb, blending your content and style with the rest of the sentence.

1. As the bull reached the cape, the man swung it alongside, ^.
   Maia Wojciechowska, Shadow of a Bull

2. The tyrannosaur's head moved close to the car, ^, and peered in.
   Michael Crichton, Jurassic Park

3. Finally, when he stood up, ^ and ^, his face was as hard and tight as wood, and his eyes were hard.
   John Steinbeck, Of Mice and Men

Using the Sentence-Composing Toolbox

CREATIVE WRITING

Revising a paragraph—To revise the plain paragraph below, at the caret marks (^) add delayed adverbs or other sentence-composing tools you've already learned.

"The Corner"

1. Jason, ^, raced out of the house into the rain, ^.
2. ^, the school bus was approaching his corner.
3. Other children, nearer the bus stop, were strolling, ^, toward that corner.
4. Under umbrellas, children huddled, ^, as they waited for its arrival.
5. The bus, ^, finally pulled up and stopped, ^.
6. ^, Jason got there just in time before it pulled away.

Write out your revision like a paragraph, not a list of sentences. Present your revised paragraph to your class to see the various effective ways you and your classmates revised the same plain paragraph to make it memorable.

Tip for Better Revising: Always, when you revise something you've written, look for places to use delayed adverbs and other sentence-composing tools to add detail, interest, and professional style to your writing.

Using the Sentence-Composing Toolbox

REVIEWING THE TOOLS: MICHAEL CRICHTON'S *JURASSIC PARK*

Directions: Using these abbreviations, identify the underlined tools. If you need to review the tool, study the pages listed below.

Words	Review These Pages
opening adjective = OADJ	pages 12–16
delayed adjective = DADJ	pages 18–22
opening adverb = OADV	pages 24–28
delayed adverb = DADV	pages 30–37

REVIEW 1: IDENTIFYING

Directions: Write the abbreviation of the underlined tool. Each sentence illustrates either an opening adjective (OADJ) or an opening adverb (OADV).

1. <u>Immediately</u>, the little lizard sprang up, leaping over Grant's head into Tim's arms.
2. <u>High in the branches</u>, he had a good view of the forest, the tops of the trees extending away to his left and right.
3. <u>Nervous at most times</u>, Arnold was especially edgy now.
4. <u>Outside</u>, lightning flashed, and there was the sharp crack of thunder.
5. <u>Then</u>, they smelled the odor of the dead goat, a garbage stench of putrefaction and decay that drifted up the hillside toward them.

Directions: Write the abbreviation of the underlined tool. Each sentence illustrates either a delayed adjective (DADJ) or a delayed adverb (DADV).

6. Amid the ferns, Grant saw the head of an animal, <u>motionless</u>, partially hidden in the fronds, the two large dark eyes watching him coldly.
7. The head of the tyrannosaur pulled away, <u>abruptly</u>.
8. The tyrannosaur's head moved close to the car, <u>sideways</u>, and peered in.
9. She was walking along, just looking around, <u>calmly</u>.
10. Moving slowly among the orderly green rectangular tables, <u>silent as a ghost except for the hissing of its breath</u>, was a velociraptor.

Using the Sentence-Composing Toolbox

REVIEW 2: IMITATING

The model sentences below contain the four tools you just reviewed—*opening adjective, opening adverb, delayed adjective, delayed adverb*—as well as other kinds of sentence-composing tools. For each model sentence, write the letter of the sentence below that imitates it. Then write your own imitation of each model.

Model Sentences:

1. He stretched out his hands, blindly, frantically, waving them in the air to ward off the attack from the dinosaur he knew was coming.
2. Big lizards like the five-foot Komodo dragons of Indonesia have been clocked at thirty miles an hour, fast enough to run down a man.
3. Ahead, Grant saw an island, rugged and craggy, rising sharply from the ocean.
4. The sound floated toward them again, soft as a sigh.
5. Abruptly, with a metallic scraping shriek, the car fell from the tyrannosaur's jaws, sickeningly, and Tim's stomach heaved in the moment before the world became totally black, and silent.

Imitations:

A. Outside, Maura heard a sound, high-pitched and shrill, coming apparently from the yard.
B. Kowalski reached for the baseball bat, uncertainly, nervously, taking it into his hands to thwart the victory of the opponents he felt was nearing.
C. Certain antique cars like the model-T Fords of Detroit have been restored at great expense to their owners, expensive enough to buy three brand-new automobiles.
D. Then, with a frenzied whirling motion, the leaves blew through the front yard, haphazardly, and Bud's conscience stirred with the thought of more work after he was so tired, and lazy.
E. The moonlight appeared on their bed nightly, lovely as candlelight.

REVIEW 3: CREATING

The paragraph below is based upon an incident in *Jurassic Park*: a tyrannosaur terrifies two children, Timmy and Lex, who have locked themselves in a Jeep.

At the caret (^), use your imagination to add opening adjectives, opening adverbs, delayed adjectives, delayed adverbs to make the paragraph good enough to appear in the original novel!

Using the Sentence-Composing Toolbox

"The Terror of the Tyrannosaurus"

(1) ^, down the hill roared the tyrannosaur, ^. (2) ^, Timmy and Lex ran toward the Jeep, jumped in, shut and locked the doors, ^. (3) ^, the beast pursued them, nearing the car that imprisoned them, then pausing at the sound of Lex, Timmy's little sister, crying inside, ^. (4) ^, thunder sounded amid the downpour, echoing the sudden ferocious high-pitched snarls of the animal. (5) With its snake-like eyes in its sinister head, the animal glared at the children through the windshield of the Jeep, ^, and Timmy and Lex, ^, screamed at the hideousness of those green slit-eyes and the sharpness of its jagged, knife-like teeth, inside its grinning mouth.

Add a few more spectacular sentences, with lots of sentence-composing tools!

Using the Sentence-Composing Toolbox

Sentence-Composing Tools: Absolute Phrase

DEFINITION

A sentence part describing the rest of the sentence in which it appears. Absolutes are *almost* complete sentences. As a test, you can make every absolute a sentence by adding *was* or *were*.

Example: He sat down at the table, **the cup in both hands**, and tried to drink.
>> Hal Borland, *When the Legends Die*

Test: The cup *was* in both hands.

Another way to identify an absolute is that often absolutes begin with these words: *my, his, her, its, our, their* (possessive pronouns). The pronoun can be stated or implied.

Examples:

Visible possessive pronoun: The old willow tree was enormous, **its sprawling branches going up like reaching arms with many long-fingered hands**. *(The word* its *is visible before* sprawling branches, *stated not implied.)*
>> J. R. R. Tolkien, *The Lord of the Rings*

Invisible possessive pronoun: An old man was standing before them, **wide, pale eyes shining like moons through the gloom of the shop**. *(The word* his *is invisible before* wide, pale eyes, *implied not stated.)*
>> J. K. Rowling, *Harry Potter and the Sorcerer's Stone*

Single Absolutes:

1. **His heart beating very fast**, Harry stood listening to the chilly silence.
   >> J. K. Rowling, *Harry Potter and the Chamber of Secrets*

2. Patrick, **book in hand**, was at another shelf, looking at English soldiers of differing periods.
   >> Lynne Reid Banks, *The Return of the Indian*

3. Radley had been leaning against the wall when I came into the room, **his arms folded across his chest**.
   >> Harper Lee, *To Kill a Mockingbird*

Using the Sentence-Composing Toolbox

Multiple Absolutes:

4. **The newcomers so forlorn**, and **the old dog team so worn out**, the outlook was anything but bright.

   Jack London, *The Call of the Wild*

5. Mr. Barnett, **his face red** and **eyes bulging**, immediately pounced on her.

   Mildred D. Taylor, *Roll of Thunder, Hear My Cry*

6. In the quiet, I heard them beyond the corral, **Cyclone barking** and **the lamb making its kind of noise** and **the ewe making her kind of noise**.

   Joseph Krumgold, *And Now Miguel*

PRACTICE 1: MATCHING

Match the absolute phrases with the sentences. Write out each sentence, inserting the absolute phrases at the caret (^) and underlining them.

Sentences:

1. ^, Billy laid the peanut-butter-and-fried-worm sandwich down on the table.

   Thomas Rockwell, *How to Eat Fried Worms*

2. Calvin, ^, did not relax his hold.

   Madeleine L'Engle, *A Wrinkle in Time*

3. At last, ^, she got up in an apologetic sort of way, and moved toward the better protected rear of the car, feeling the empty seats as she went in search for hot pipes.

   Henry Sydnor Harrison, "Miss Hinch"

4. ^, the young dog gave chase, swerving and turning in pursuit, but always the rabbit was just out of reach of his hungry jaws.

   Sheila Burnford, *The Incredible Journey*

Absolutes:

a. their little shoulders hunched

b. head down, tail flying

c. his hand trembling

d. face screwed up with grim determination

Using the Sentence-Composing Toolbox

5. Soon, the crowd of gnomes in the field started walking away in a staggering line, ^.

    e. her teeth chattering

    J. K. Rowling, *Harry Potter and the Chamber of Secrets*

PRACTICE 2: UNSCRAMBLING TO IMITATE

In the model and the scrambled list, identify the absolute phrase. Next, unscramble and write out the sentence parts to imitate the model. Finally, write your own imitation of the model and identify the absolute phrase.

MODEL: The raptor struck out with its hind claws, and with a single swift movement ripped open the belly of the fallen animal, coils of intestine falling out, like fat snakes.

Michael Crichton, Jurassic Park

a. took down the tree in the front yard

b. pieces of branches blowing everywhere

c. and in the very first moment

d. like crazy arrows

e. the storm broke out with a lightning crack

PRACTICE 3: COMBINING TO IMITATE

In the model, identify the absolute phrases. Next, combine the list of sentences to imitate the model. Finally, write your own imitation of the model and identify the absolute phrases.

MODEL: They all fell silent, the hobbit standing by the grey stone and the dwarves watching impatiently.

J. R. R. Tolkien, The Hobbit

a. The victors all became frenzied.

b. The fans were yelling from their bleachers.

c. And the players were cheering deafeningly.

Using the Sentence-Composing Toolbox

PRACTICE 4: IMITATING

Identify the absolutes in the models and sample imitations. Then choose one of the models and write an imitation of the entire sentence, one sentence part at a time. See if your classmates can guess your model.

Models:

1. Washed and refreshed, the hobbits were seated at the table, two on each side.
   J. R. R. Tolkien, The Lord of the Rings

   Sample: Coached and conditioned, the finalists were standing at the high diving board, Albert at the head.

2. There, his black robes rippling in a cold breeze, stood Severus Snape.
   J. K. Rowling, Harry Potter and the Chamber of Secrets

   Sample: Upside down, his loose change falling from his pants pocket, dangled Devon Smith.

3. Charles Wallace, in yellow footed pajamas, his fresh wounds band-aided, his small nose looking puffy and red, lay on the foot of Meg's big brass bed, his head pillowed on the shiny black bulk of Fortinbras the dog.
   Madeleine L'Engle, A Wind in the Door

   Sample: The trick-or-treater, in knight's regalia, his sword unsheathed, his dashing costume appearing authentic and colorful, stood on the doorstep of the next-door neighbor's house, his finger pressed on the little doorbell of Mrs. Jackson the neighbor.

PRACTICE 5: EXPANDING

Below are sentences with the absolute phrases omitted at the caret mark (^). For each caret, add an absolute phrase, blending your content and style with the rest of the sentence.

1. This was a room about fifteen feet by twenty-five, ^.
   John Christopher, The Guardians

2. The skeleton I had uncovered lay curled on its side, ^.
   R. L. Stine, Ghost Beach

Using the Sentence-Composing Toolbox

3. For a few seconds, Harry and his Uncle Vernon, with hands around Harry's neck, struggled, ^, ^. *(Add two absolute phrases.)*

   J. K. Rowling, *Harry Potter and the Order of the Phoenix*

CREATIVE WRITING

Composing a Paragraph—Pretend that you are one of the professional writers listed below who has written the first sentence of a long story. Use one of the sentences as the first sentence in a paragraph that will begin that story. Create the rest of the paragraph. Just as the writers' sentences use absolute phrases, within your paragraph use absolute phrases and other sentence-composing tools you've learned to make your paragraph memorable.

Reminder: Don't try to write a complete story. Write only the first paragraph of that story. (Maybe later you'll want to write the entire story!)

1. The creatures, **some sitting on chairs, others reclining on a sofa**, were all watching him intently.

   Roald Dahl, *James and the Giant Peach*

2. A wild-eyed horse, **its bridle torn and dangling**, trotted frantically through the mounds of men, tossing its head, whinnying in panic.

   Lois Lowry, *The Giver*

3. There was a bespectacled boy of about eleven, and a girl a few years younger, perhaps seven or eight, **her blond hair pushed up under a baseball cap**, and **a baseball glove slung over her shoulder**.

   Michael Crichton, *Jurassic Park*

Using the Sentence-Composing Toolbox

Sentence-Composing Tools: Appositive Phrase

DEFINITION

A noun phrase identifying a person, place, or thing named in a sentence. Appositives often begin with the words *a*, *an*, or *the*. They always answer one of these questions:

    Who is he? Who is she? Who are they? *(people)*
    What is it? What are they? *(places or things)*

Examples:

Identifying people: Don Gross was a tough guy, **an ex-Marine who had never lost his military manner.**

    Michael Crichton, *Prey*

Identifying places: Once they were in her office, **a small room with a large, welcoming fire**, Professor McGonagall motioned to Harry and Hermione to sit down.

    J. K. Rowling, *Harry Potter and the Prisoner of Azkaban*

Identifying things: When it was quite late, he murmured something, went to a closet, and drew forth an evil weapon, **a long yellowish tube ending in bellows and a trigger.**

    Ray Bradbury, *The Martian Chronicles*

Single Appositives:

1. **A balding, smooth-faced man,** he could have been anywhere between forty and sixty.

    Harper Lee, *To Kill a Mockingbird*

2. Lou Epstein, **the oldest, shortest, and baldest of the three Epstein brothers,** barely looked up from the cash register when Alfred entered the store.

    Robert Lipsyte, *The Contender*

3. In the locker room, I packed for the trip to New Orleans, **the road-trip that would change my life and destiny as an athlete forever.**

    Pat Conroy, *My Losing Season*

Using the Sentence-Composing Toolbox

Multiple Appositives:

4. In New York, **the most important state in any Presidential race,** and **a state where politics were particularly sensitive to the views of various nationality and minority groups,** Democrats were joyous and Republicans angry and gloomy.

    John F. Kennedy, *Profiles in Courage*

5. The dawn came quickly now, **a wash, a glow, a lightness,** and then **an explosion of fire,** as the sun arose out of the Gulf.

    John Steinbeck, *The Pearl*

6. Beneath the dragon, under all his limbs and his huge coiled tail, and about him on all sides stretching away across the unseen floors, lay countless piles of precious things, **gold wrought and unwrought, gems and jewels,** and **silver red-stained in the ruddy light.**

    J. R. R. Tolkien, *The Hobbit*

PRACTICE 1: MATCHING

Match the appositive phrases with the sentences. Write out each sentence, inserting the appositive phrases at the caret (^) and underlining them.

Sentences:

1. ^, he reminded me of a baby bird.
    Tracy Chevalier, *Girl with a Pearl Earring*

2. Tom Grieves, ^, named the birds Peter Soil and Maggie Mess.
    Frank B. Gilbreth, Jr. and Ernestine Gilbreth Carey, *Cheaper by the Dozen*

3. From every hill slope came the trickle of running water, ^.
    Jack London, *The Call of the Wild*

4. ^, the North Star would soon be visible and would point the way when the birds had all gone South.
    Jean Craighead George, *Julie of the Wolves*

Appositives:

a. a box with dials and a small light shining on the front

b. the music of unseen fountains

c. the guidepost of her ancestors

d. a bald little man

Using the Sentence-Composing Toolbox

5. What attracted Mrs. Frisby's attention the most was a box in one corner of the room, ^.
       Robert C. O'Brien, *Mrs. Frisby and the Rats of NIMH*

   e. the handyman who had to clean up the cage

PRACTICE 2: UNSCRAMBLING TO IMITATE

In the model and the scrambled list, identify the appositive phrase. Next, unscramble and write out the sentence parts to imitate the model. Finally, write your own imitation of the model and identify the appositive phrase.

MODEL: Fudge, a portly little man in a long, pinstriped cloak, looked cold and exhausted.
    J. K. Rowling, *Harry Potter and the Prisoner of Azkaban*

a. Nora was a sickly gray-haired woman in a shabby blue blouse.

b. She seemed surprised.

c. But she was grateful.

PRACTICE 3: COMBINING TO IMITATE

In the model, identify the appositive phrase. Next, combine the list of sentences to imitate the model. Finally, write your own imitation of the model and identify the appositive phrase.

MODEL: Gilly gave little William Ernest the most fearful face in all her collection of scary looks, a cross between Count Dracula and Godzilla.
    Katherine Paterson, *The Great Gilly Hopkins*

a. Stephen gave his big sister Karen something.

b. He gave her some tasty candies.

c. They were from his birthday party at the mall.

d. They were an assortment of creams and caramels.

Using the Sentence-Composing Toolbox

PRACTICE 4: IMITATING

Identify the appositives in the models and sample imitations. Then choose one of the models and write an imitation of the entire sentence, one sentence part at a time. See if your classmates can guess your model.

Models:

1. A veteran bronc rider, Tom Black had ridden nine horses to death in the rodeo arena, and at every performance the spectators expected him to kill another one.

    Hal Borland, *When the Legends Die*

    Sample: An experienced scuba diver, Chrissy Gibson had gone on ten expeditions to unexplored areas of the Caribbean, and on each dive she forced herself to chart new underwater territory.

2. Fred Stewart, a thin, wiry little man with sunken cheeks and red-rimmed eyes, met them.

    Laurence E. Stotz, "Fire"

    Sample: Erin O'Connor, a surprised, overjoyed eighth grader, with bright eyes and cornstalk hair, won the contest.

3. From every hill slope came the trickle of running water, the music of unseen fountains.

    Jack London, *The Call of the Wild*

    Sample: In each wrapped box was a pair of lovely shoes, the gift of a generous company.

PRACTICE 5: EXPANDING

Below are sentences with the appositive phrases omitted at the caret mark (^). For each caret, add an appositive phrase, blending your content and style with the rest of the sentence.

1. Finally he found what he was looking for, ^.

    Hal Borland, *When the Legends Die*

Using the Sentence-Composing Toolbox

2. ^, he took little interest in troublesome things, preferring to remain on good terms with everyone.
   Mildred D. Taylor, *Roll of Thunder, Hear My Cry*

3. He could see the furniture in his room, ^, and he got up and went downstairs in his pajamas to see if he was right about what would be waiting there.
   Lois Duncan, *A Gift of Magic*

CREATIVE WRITING

Revising a paragraph—To revise the plain paragraph below, at the caret marks (^) add appositive phrases and other sentence-composing tools you've already learned.

"Her World"

1. She looked around her room, the ^, at what she owned.
2. A ^, the oversized stuffed animal was one of her favorite possessions.
3. On the wall was a large poster, one that ^.
4. Her book bag, the ^, was on a shelf.
5. On a hook on the the back of her door hung her party dress, a ^.
6. She knew that her favorite party shoes, a pair of ^, were under the bed.

Write out your revision like a paragraph, not a list of sentences. Present your revised paragraph to your class to see the various effective ways you and your classmates revised the same plain paragraph to make it memorable.

Tips for Better Revising: Always, when you revise something you've written, look for places to use appositive phrases and other sentence-composing tools to add detail, interest, and professional style to your writing.

Using the Sentence-Composing Toolbox

Sentence-Composing Tools: Prepositional Phrase

DEFINITION

A preposition is the first word in a prepositional phrase. Here are common prepositions: *about, above, across, after, along, at, before, behind, below, beyond, by, down, except, from, in, inside, like, near, off, on, over, outside, to, through, under, up, upon, with, within, without.*

Any word that will fit in this blank is a preposition: It was ____ the box; *about the box, at the box, beyond the box, from the box, near the box, over the box, under the box, inside the box, outside the box, by the box,* and so on.

Prepositional phrases can be *single, connected (a series of two or more in a row),* or *multiple* (two or more in the same position but—unlike connected phrases—separated by commas).

Examples:

Single prepositional phrase: **On the whole enormous prairie,** there was no sign that any other human being had ever been there.

Laura Ingalls Wilder, Little House on the Prairie

Connected prepositional phrases: **Upon the grass of the great plains,** the crooked, bare old thorn trees were scattered. *(a series of two connected prepositional phrases:* **upon the grass** *and* **of the great plains.***)*

Isak Dinesen, Out of Africa

Multiple prepositional phrases: **Behind a billboard, on an empty lot,** he opened the purse and saw a pile of silver and copper coins. *(two in the same position, separated by commas)*

Charles Spencer Chaplin, My Autobiography

Single or Connected Prepositional Phrases:

1. **On the far side of the camping ground,** just where the trees began, they saw the Lion slowly walking away **from them into the wood.**

   C. S. Lewis, The Chronicles of Narnia

2. The class buildings, **with their backs against the forest wall,** formed a semicircle facing a small one-room church **at the opposite end of the compound.**

   Mildred D. Taylor, Roll of Thunder, Hear My Cry

Using the Sentence-Composing Toolbox

3. **Except for church on Sundays or a rare outing**, she spent most **of her days** alone listening **to her little Philco radio** and had learned to sing just about every song she heard.

    Fannie Flagg, *Standing in the Rainbow*

Multiple Prepositional Phrases in Same Position:

4. They tiptoed from room to room, afraid to speak above a whisper and gazing with a kind of awe **at the unbelievable luxury, at the beds with their feather mattresses, the looking-glasses, the horsehair sofa, the Brussels carpet, the lithograph of Queen Victoria over the drawing-room mantelpiece.**

    George Orwell, *Animal Farm*

5. **To his home, to his comfort, to the bringing up of their children, to the garden and her greenhouse, to the local church, and to her patchwork quilts**, Margaret had happily given her life.

    P. D. James, *A Certain Justice*

6. Janet and the Tiger went racing back, **over the country** and **over the town, over houses and churches and mountains and rivers, across the park** and **along the street**, and **in Janet's window**.

    Joan Aiken, "A Necklace of Raindrops"

PRACTICE 1: MATCHING

Match the prepositional phrases with the sentences. Write out each sentence, inserting the prepositional phrases at the caret (^) and underlining them.

Sentences:

1. ^, he had forgotten all his troubles.

    Mark Twain, *The Adventures of Tom Sawyer*

2. The man in black, ^, galloped up to the wall gate and disappeared like a great dark shadow.

    Post Wheeler, *Vasilissa the Beautiful*

Prepositions:

a. with no movement in the wide and lonely land

b. around the long table

Using the Sentence-Composing Toolbox

3. The morning was still, ^.
   William Barrett, *The Lilies of the Field*

4. ^, when he was sure everybody in the settlement would be asleep, Brandon left the cabin and ran swiftly as a young deer into the protecting shadows of the woods.
   Madeleine L'Engle, *A Swiftly Tilting Planet*

5. There, ^, sat half a dozen farmers and half a dozen of the more eminent pigs, Napoleon himself occupying the seat of honor at the head of the table.
   George Orwell, *Animal Farm*

c. within two minutes, or even less

d. in the small hours of the morning, before dawn

e. on a coal-black horse

PRACTICE 2: UNSCRAMBLING TO IMITATE

In the model and the scrambled list, identify the prepositional phrase. Next, unscramble and write out the sentence parts to imitate the model. Finally, write your own imitation of the model and identify the prepositional phrase.

MODEL: The pebble was flaming red, shiny, and perfectly round, like a marble.
   William Steig, "Sylvester and the Magic Pebble"

a. The snake was bright green.
b. The snake was tiny.
c. And the snake was very thin.
d. The snake was like a shoelace.

PRACTICE 3: COMBINING TO IMITATE

In the model, identify the prepositional phrases. Next, combine the list of sentences to imitate the model. Finally, write your own imitation of the model and identify the prepositional phrases.

Using the Sentence-Composing Toolbox

MODEL: Janet and the Tiger went racing back, over the country and over the town, over houses and churches and mountains and rivers, across the park and along the street.

Joan Aiken, "A Necklace of Raindrops"

a. Alfred and his brother started going home.

b. They went across the railroad tracks and across the empty lot.

c. They went past warehouses and businesses and cars and corners.

d. They went along the canal and toward the bridge.

PRACTICE 4: IMITATING

Identify the prepositional phrases in the models and sample imitations. Then choose one of the models and write an imitation of the entire sentence, one sentence part at a time. See if your classmates can guess your model.

Models:

1. In all that space of land and sky stood the lonely, small, covered wagon.

Laura Ingalls Wilder, *Little House on the Prairie*

   Sample: In every few hours of practice and training came a slight, certain, speed improvement.

2. Brendon, in his room at the end of the hall, still slept, breathing through his mouth with a little snorting sound that meant he was soon to waken.

Lois Duncan, *A Gift of Magic*

   Sample: Porky, in his split-second decision about strategy at the scrimmage line, suddenly turned, running through the linebackers with a huge quick power surge that signaled he was about to score.

3. The fire made him think of home, of food and warmth and company, of faces around the evening circle, of the drone of old men's voices, telling their endless tales of daring.

Armstrong Sperry, *Call It Courage*

   Sample: The ocean made Jenny think of vacation, of summer and swimming and relaxing, of lounging on her beach chair, of the joy of laughter of small children, playing their beach games with squeals.

Using the Sentence-Composing Toolbox

PRACTICE 5: EXPANDING

Below are sentences with the prepositional phrases omitted at the caret mark (^). For each caret, add a prepositional phrase, blending your content and style with the rest of the sentence.

1. ^, she was glad to be in the quiet hospital room.

   Eleanor Coerr, *Sadako and the Thousand Paper Cranes*

2. Jonas, ^, searched the auditorium for a glimpse of his father.

   Lois Lowry, *The Giver*

3. Terrified, Bilbo tried to run faster, but suddenly he struck his toes on a snag in the floor, and fell flat, ^.

   J. R. R. Tolkien, *The Hobbit*

CREATIVE WRITING

Composing a paragraph—Pretend that you are one of the professional writers below who has written the first sentence of a long story. Use one of the sentences as the first sentence in a paragraph that will begin that story. Create the rest of the paragraph. Just as the writers' sentences use prepositional phrases, within your paragraph use prepositional phrases and other sentence-composing tools you've learned to make your paragraph memorable.

Reminder: Don't try to write a complete story. Write only the first paragraph of that story! (Maybe later you'll want to write the entire story!)

1. **All around us**, dead fruit trees rose **like ghostly hands**.

   Laurence Yep, *Dragon of the Lost Sea*

2. That moment **of utter darkness, at the height of the storm**, was one **of the most terrifying** Johnny had ever experienced.

   Arthur C. Clarke, *Dolphin Island*

3. He heard a low hissing sound, **like a very large snake**.

   Michael Crichton, *Jurassic Park*

Using the Sentence-Composing Toolbox

Sentence-Composing Tools: Participial Phrase

DEFINITION

A verbal ending in *-ing* or *-ed* used to describe. A verbal is a verb that also works like another part of speech. Participles show action, so they act like verbs, but they also describe, so they act like adjectives.

Present participles always end in *ing*. Unlike *ing* main verbs, which cannot be removed from a sentence, participles are removable.

Examples:

Verb (not removable): Harry was **feeling slightly more cheerful**.

Present participle (verbal, removable): **Feeling slightly more cheerful**, Harry helped himself to sausages and fried tomatoes.

     J. K. Rowling, *Harry Potter and the Prisoner of Azkaban*

Difference Between Present Participles and Gerunds: Like present participles, gerunds (page 62) are verbals that also end in *ing*, but it's easy to tell the difference between gerunds and present participles. Present participles are removable sentence parts; gerunds are not. In each sample pair that follows the first contains a present participle, and the second contains a gerund. Notice that only the present participles can be removed.

1a. **Feeling so much better after the nap**, Gunster dressed and went out.

1b. **Feeling so much better after the nap** relieved Gunster.

2a. Ralston, **going down the staircase backward**, was very unsteady.

2b. The cause of Ralston's fall was **going down the staircase backward**.

3a. The damaged plane landed poorly, **skidding left and right with sparks flying everywhere**.

3b. The captain during touchdown worried about **skidding left and right with sparks flying everywhere**.

Past participles usually end in *ed*. Unlike *ed* main verbs, which cannot be removed from a sentence, past participles are removable. (*Note:* Most past participles end in *ed*; others—by far the minority—end in *en (forgiven)* or end irregularly *(sung)*. This book treats only the most common—those with *ed*—because once you learn the *ed* participles, you will intuit and use the others.)

Using the Sentence-Composing Toolbox

Examples:

Verb (not removable): The bats were **wrapped in their brown wings**.

Past participle (verbal, removable): High up under the roof, in the farthest corner of the barn, the bats were hanging upside down, **wrapped in their brown wings**.
Randal Jarrell, The Bat Poet

Good writers sometimes use multiple participles within the same sentence.

Examples:

Present participles: He had sailed for two hours, **resting in the stern** and **chewing a bit of the meat from the marlin, trying to rest and to be strong**, when he saw the first of the two sharks. *(three)*
Ernest Hemingway, The Old Man and the Sea

Past participles: The master, **throned on high in his splint-bottomed armchair**, was dozing, **lulled by the drowsy hum of study**. *(two)*
Mark Twain, The Adventures of Tom Sawyer

Both present and past participles: He sat by the windows, **hunched down in a rocking chair, scowling, waiting**. *(one past participle and two present participles)*
Harper Lee, To Kill a Mockingbird

Single Participles:

1. **Buried in a nearby leather armchair**, Spencer V. Silverthorne, a young buyer for Nuget's department store, slumbered.
   Walter Lord, A Night to Remember

2. The crocodile, **pretending to be a harmless log**, glided silently toward her until, without the slightest warning, it intended to snap its powerful jaws over her head.
   Rani Manicka, The Rice Mother

3. A woman stood on her back step, arms folded, **waiting**.
   Doris Lessing, The Summer Before Dark

Using the Sentence-Composing Toolbox

Multiple Participles:

4. **Clapping** and **stepping in unison**, our group moved away from the swarms, which thrummed deeply and followed.

    Michael Crichton, *Prey*

5. Our father, **dreaming bitterly of Barbados, despised** and **mocked by his neighbors** and **ignored by his sons**, held down his unspeakable factory job, spread his black gospel in bars on the weekend, and drank his rum.

    James Baldwin, *Tell Me How Long the Train's Been Gone*

6. **Swollen to the top of its banks, clouded dark brown with silt, belching dirt and stones,** and **carrying blown branches along in its torrent**, it had turned into an ugly, angered river.

    Bill and Vera Cleaver, *Where the Lilies Bloom*

PRACTICE 1: MATCHING

Match the participial phrases with the sentences. Write out each sentence, inserting the participial phrases at the caret (^) and underlining them.

Sentences:

1. ^, Pollard, the jockey, swung Seabiscuit clear of a set of chain-reaction collisions on the far turn.

    Laura Hillenbrand, *Seabiscuit: An American Legend*

2. The penguins, ^, looked curiously at Mr. Greenbaum.

    Richard and Florence Atwater, *Mr. Popper's Penguins*

3. In the other narrow bed, his brother Eugene, unaware, went on sleeping, ^.

    Gina Berriault, "The Stone Boy"

4. They dressed the bear, ^.

    Paula Fox, *Maurice's Room*

Participles:

a. pulling Jacob's hat almost all the way down its muzzle

b. mounted on high-stepping horses

c. fighting his way through one of the wildest races of the season

d. undisturbed by the alarm clock's rusty ring

Using the Sentence-Composing Toolbox

5. ^, a pair of soldiers were advancing along the river road.

    Sid Fleischman, *The Whipping Boy*

e. standing politely in two rows of six each

PRACTICE 2: UNSCRAMBLING TO IMITATE

In the model and the scrambled list, identify the participial phrases (one past, one present). Next, unscramble and write out the sentence parts to imitate the model. Finally, write your own imitation of the model and identify the participial phrases (one past, one present).

MODEL: The dinosaur had spit into his eye with acidy foam, and as he realized it, the pain overwhelmed him, and he dropped to his knees, disoriented completely, wheezing breathlessly.

    Michael Crichton, *Jurassic Park*

a. and when he saw this

b. intensely focused, breathing hard

c. his determination took over

d. and he picked up his pace

e. the runner had passed him on his left with surprising speed

PRACTICE 3: COMBINING TO IMITATE

In the model, identify the participial phrases (present and past). Next, combine the list of sentences to imitate the model. Finally, write your own imitation of the model and identify the participial phrases (present and past).

MODEL: Hating himself, repulsed by what he was doing, Harry forced the goblet back toward Dumbledore's mouth and tipped it for Dumbledore to drink the remainder of the horrible potion inside.

    J. K. Rowling, *Harry Potter and the Half-Blood Prince*

a. He was gripping his dog's head.

b. He was concerned about what the dog was feeling.

c. Don opened Lucky's mouth wide for the medicine.

Using the Sentence-Composing Toolbox

d. And Don lowered the bottle.

e. Don lowered it for his dog to take the last of the remaining dose within.

PRACTICE 4: IMITATING

Identify the participles (past and present) in the models and sample imitations. Then choose one of the models and write an imitation of the entire sentence, one sentence part at a time. See if your classmates can guess your model.

Models:

1. Chagrined, Ramona tore down her sign, crumpled it, threw it into the fireplace, and stalked out of the room, resolving to do better the next time.

   Beverly Cleary, *Ramona and Her Father*

   Sample: Brokenhearted, Henrietta took off the ring, smashed it, threw it into the trash can, and darted away from her boyfriend, hoping to put distance between them.

2. Creeping without sound through the underbrush, he at last came to a thicket at the very edge of the water, and parting the leaves with careful hands, he beheld a most beautiful sight.

   Elizabeth Coatsworth, "The Story of Wang Li"

   Sample: Huffing with breathlessness throughout the chore, he finally arrived at the end of the garden at the far corner of the yard, and pulling out remaining weeds with a special tool, he finished the very tiresome job.

3. For a long time, he just stood there, defeated, listening to the hammer, hoping the chopper would come back, but knowing that it would not.

   Robb White, *Deathwatch*

   Sample: During the entire morning, she just stayed home, worried, waiting for the call, hoping the phone would ring, but fearing that it would not.

PRACTICE 5: EXPANDING

Below are sentences with the participial phrases omitted at the caret mark (^). For each caret, add a participial phrase (present or past), blending your content and style with the rest of the sentence.

Using the Sentence-Composing Toolbox

1. ^, ^, was a cloaked figure that towered to the ceiling.
    J. K. Rowling, *Harry Potter and the Prisoner of Azkaban*

2. Against all the four walls of the great room, ^ and ^, were thousands and thousands of the finest and fattest ducks and geese, ^.
    Roald Dahl, *Fantastic Mr. Fox*

3. ^, ^, ^, ^, strode Calvin.
    Rosa Guy, *The Friends*

CREATIVE WRITING

Revising a paragraph—To revise the plain paragraph below, at the caret marks (^) add present or past participial phrases or other sentence-composing tools you've already learned.

"Crime Scene Investigation"

1. ^, the detective arrived on the crime scene.
2. He talked to two policemen, ^.
3. Then, ^, he went over to the shattered window.
4. He examined it, ^.
5. ^, he dusted for fingerprints.
6. The crime lab photographer, ^, took pictures.

Write out your revision like a paragraph, not a list of sentences. Present your revised paragraph to your class to see the various effective ways you and your classmates revised the same plain paragraph to make it memorable.

Tip for Better Revising: Always, when you revise something you've written, look for places to use present and past participial phrases and other sentence-composing tools to add detail, interest, and professional style to your writing.

Using the Sentence-Composing Toolbox

Sentence-Composing Tools: Gerund Phrase

DEFINITION

A verbal ending in *-ing* used to name activities. A verbal is a verb that also works like another part of speech. Gerunds show action, so they act like verbs, but they also name, so they act like nouns by naming activities.

To see how gerunds act like nouns, insert any of these gerunds into any of the blanks: *playing chess, learning new things, climbing mountains in distant lands, building sand castles on the beach, taking a computer apart to investigate its guts,* and so on.

1. _____ is fun. *(subject)*
2. We like _____. *(direct object)*
3. They talked about _____. *(object of preposition)*
4. A great leisure activity is _____. *(predicate noun)*
5. Their favorite pastime, _____, is enjoyed by many. *(appositive)*

Difference Between Present Participles and Gerunds: Like gerunds, present participles (page 56) are verbals that also end in *ing,* but it's easy to tell the difference between them and gerunds. Present participles can be removed from the sentence without destroying the sentence, but gerunds cannot be removed without destroying the sentence. In each sample pair that follows, the first contains a present participle, and the second contains a gerund. Notice that only the present participles can be removed.

1a. **Feeling so much better after the nap**, Gunster dressed and went out.

1b. **Feeling so much better after the nap** relieved Gunster.

2a. Ricky, **going down the staircase backward**, was very unsteady.

2b. His mom had warned Ricky about **going down the staircase backward**.

3a. The damaged plane landed poorly, **skidding left and right with sparks flying everywhere.**

3b. The captain during touchdown worried about **skidding left and right with sparks flying everywhere.**

Single Gerunds:

1. **Pushing the handcart up to the man's house** was tiring.

   John Hersey, *Hiroshima*

Using the Sentence-Composing Toolbox

2. After **making ten birds**, Sadako lined them up on the table beside the golden crane.

    Eleanor Coerr, *Sadako and the Thousand Paper Cranes*

3. He started **waking up before the alarm that week fresher in the morning and stronger**.

    Robert Lipsyte, *The Contender*

Multiple Gerunds:

4. Love does not consist in **gazing at each other** but in **looking outward together in the same direction**.

    Antoine de Saint-Exupéry, *The Little Prince*

5. He believed the only three valid purposes microwaves served were **re-heating coffee**, **making popcorn**, and **putting some heat on take-out from places like Cluck-Cluck Tonite**.

    Stephen King, *Needful Things*

6. He kept **slipping into deep drifts of snow**, and **skidding on frozen puddles**, and **tripping over fallen tree trunks**, and **sliding down steep banks**, and **barking his shins against rocks** until he was wet and cold and bruised all over.

    C. S. Lewis, *The Chronicles of Narnia*

PRACTICE 1: MATCHING

Match the gerund phrases with the sentences. Write out each sentence, inserting the gerund phrases at the caret (^) and underlining them.

Sentences:

1. Before ^, I always closed the closet door.

    Mercer Mayer, *There's a Nightmare in My Closet*

2. Eventually, Mr. Kato fired a shot into the dark one night, after ^.

    John Steinbeck, *The Red Pony*

Gerunds:

a. conjuring up portable, waterproof fires

b. putting their plastic figures into the magic cupboard, by turning the magic key

Using the Sentence-Composing Toolbox

3. ^ was a specialty of Hermione's.   c. bathing
   J. K. Rowling, *Harry Potter and the Chamber of Secrets*

4. For ^, John used a bucket.   d. seeing a face looking in his window
   Joseph Krumgold, *Onion John*

5. By ^, Omri had the power to recall them to life.   e. going to sleep
   Lynne Reid Banks, *The Return of the Indian*

PRACTICE 2: UNSCRAMBLING TO IMITATE

In the model and the scrambled list, identify the gerund phrase. Next, unscramble and write out the sentence parts to imitate the model. Finally, write your own imitation of the model and identify the gerund phrase.

MODEL: Saddling the pony the first time was a ticklish job.
John Steinbeck, *The Red Pony*

a. each morning

b. is a pleasant routine

c. bathing the baby

PRACTICE 3: COMBINING TO IMITATE

In the model, identify the gerund phrases. Next, combine the list of sentences to imitate the model. Finally, write your own imitation of the model and identify the gerund phrases.

MODEL: Spraying bright colors, dancing, and singing are all part of the excitement.
Charles R. Joy, "Hindu Girl of Surinam"

a. Throwing touchdown balls is a responsibility of the quarterback.

b. Running is a responsibility of the quarterback.

c. And passing is a responsibility of the quarterback.

Using the Sentence-Composing Toolbox

PRACTICE 4: IMITATING

Identify the gerunds in the models and sample imitations. Then choose one of the models and write an imitation of the entire sentence, one sentence part at a time. See if your classmates can guess your model.

Models:

1. Delivering a short talk made him word-conscious, and learning current events strengthened his memory.
   Harper Lee, *To Kill a Mockingbird*

   Sample: Jumping in the autumn leaves made her giggle, and drinking hot chocolate restored her energy.

2. Walking across fields with Onion John and into woods was as good as going for a hike through a mail order catalog.
   Joseph Krumgold, *Onion John*

   Sample: Talking about problems with her best friend and about solutions was as helpful as listening to a counselor in the guidance office.

3. He drove on another mile before stopping again, climbing out, carrying his lunch bucket, and walking to a little hill where he could look back at the dusty city.
   Ray Bradbury, *The Martian Chronicles*

   Sample: The car continued on another lap before faltering once, spinning suddenly, losing its traction, and overturning near the guard rail where it finally stopped without an explosion.

PRACTICE 5: EXPANDING

Below are sentences with the gerund phrases omitted at the caret mark (^). For each caret, add a gerund phrase, blending your content and style with the rest of the sentence.

1. ^ didn't have to stop because you got grown-up.
   Olive Ann Burns, *Cold Sassy Tree*

2. At the thought of ^ and of ^, he shuddered.
   Elliott Merrick, "Without Words"

3. He started ^ and ^, ^, ^.
   Robb White, *Deathwatch*

Using the Sentence-Composing Toolbox

CREATIVE WRITING

Composing a paragraph—Pretend that you are one of the professional writers listed below who has written the first sentence of a long story. Use one of the sentences as the first sentence in a paragraph that will begin that story. Create the rest of the paragraph. Within your paragraph use gerunds and other sentence-composing tools you've learned to make your paragraph memorable.

Reminder: Don't try to write a complete story. Write only the first paragraph of that story. (Maybe later you'll want to write the entire story!)

1. After **hovering uncertainly in the air**, the plane settled clumsily on the ground, stumbled to a stop, and then waddled into the brightly lighted area round the terminal building.

   Robert Bingham, "The Unpopular Passenger"

2. He found a pair of socks under his bed and, after **pulling a spider off one of them**, put them on.

   J. K. Rowling, *Harry Potter and the Sorcerer's Stone*

3. The pony liked short trips and showed it by **keeping his head very high** and by **quivering his nostrils with interest**.

   John Steinbeck, *The Red Pony*

Using the Sentence-Composing Toolbox

Sentence-Composing Tools: Infinitive Phrase

DEFINITION

A verbal that always begins with *to* plus a verb: *to sing, to read, to linger, to laugh, to sigh, to study,* and so on. A verbal is a verb that also works like another part of speech—a noun, an adjective, or an adverb.

Infinitives can name something (like nouns), describe something (like adjectives), or give a reason for something (like adverbs). Infinitives convey action, so they act like verbs, but at the same time they also act like nouns, adjectives, or adverbs.

Examples:

1. **To make it to the final round of the playoffs** was the team's goal. *(The noun infinitive names the team's goal.)*

2. The coach emphasized the need **to make it to the final round of the playoffs**. *(The adjective infinitive describes the need.)*

3. The team from Western High School worked overtime **to make it to the final round of the playoffs**. *(The adverb infinitive states the reason the team worked overtime.)*

Single Infinitives:

1. **To get his feet wet in such a freezing temperature** meant trouble and danger. *(noun infinitive—names what meant trouble and danger)*
   Jack London, "To Build a Fire"

2. Suddenly, she had an almost overwhelming desire **to see what was behind the other doors and down the other corridors**. *(adjective infinitive—describes desire)*
   Hal Borland, *When the Legends Die*

3. Back through the vegetable garden he went, and he paused for a moment **to smash a green muskmelon with his heel**, but he was not happy about it. *(adverb infinitive—states the reason he paused)*
   John Steinbeck, *The Red Pony*

Multiple Infinitives:

4. At nine o'clock Earth started **to explode, to catch fire, and to burn**. *(noun infinitives—name what started)*
   Ray Bradbury, *The Martian Chronicles*

Using the Sentence-Composing Toolbox

5. It was the time **to accomplish his mission** or **to fail**. *(adjective infinitives—describe the time)*

    Walter Dean Myers, *Legend of Tarik*

6. She lingered a moment or two **to bathe her own face with the cool water** and **to smooth her hair**. *(adverb infinitives—state the reason why she lingered)*

    Gaston Leroux, *The Phantom of the Opera*

PRACTICE 1: MATCHING

Match the infinitive phrases with the sentences. Write out each sentence, inserting the infinitive phrases at the caret (^) and underlining them.

Sentences:

1. ^, Aunt Petunia had insisted that the whole family follow the same diet, too.

    J. K. Rowling, *Harry Potter and the Goblet of Fire*

2. Take care to get what you like, or you will be forced to ^.

    George Bernard Shaw *(saying)*

3. All Old Yeller did was come bounding in ^.

    Fred Gipson, *Old Yeller*

4. ^, Stuart had to climb a tiny rope ladder which his father had fixed for him.

    E. B. White, *Stuart Little*

5. Hours later, walking home, my boots crunching on the snow, I bent my head backward ^.

    Katherine Paterson, *Jacob Have I Loved*

Infinitives:

a. to get to the washbasin

b. to make Dudley feel better about eating "rabbit food"

c. to like what you get

d. to drink in the crystal stars

e. to jump on us and lick us in the face and bark so loud that there, inside the cabin, the noise nearly made us deaf

69

Using the Sentence-Composing Toolbox

PRACTICE 2: UNSCRAMBLING TO IMITATE

In the model and the scrambled list, identify the infinitive phrases. Next, unscramble and write out the sentence parts to imitate the model. Finally, write your own imitation of the model and identify the infinitive phrases.

MODEL: To add to his distress, he had been badly sunburned during the day, and he kept twisting and turning on the raft in a vain attempt to find a comfortable position.
Arthur C. Clarke, Dolphin Island

a. in an effort to attract the team's sympathy

b. she had been loudly yelled at after the game

c. and she continued sobbing and moaning in the locker room

d. to exaggerate the drama

PRACTICE 3: COMBINING TO IMITATE

In the model, identify the infinitive phrase. Next, combine the list of sentences to imitate the model. Finally, write your own imitation of the model and identify the infinitive phrase.

MODEL: To qualify for the racing team in junior high, she had to practice every day.
Eleanor Coerr, Sadako and the Thousand Paper Cranes

a. He needed to do something to participate in the pie eating contest.

b. The pie eating contest was at the school fair.

c. What he needed to do was to stop eating the day before.

PRACTICE 4: IMITATING

Identify the infinitives in the models and sample imitations. Then choose one of the models and write an imitation of the entire sentence, one sentence part at a time. See if your classmates can guess your model.

Models:

1. I learned to respect the past, to respect my own heritage and myself.
Mildred D. Taylor, Roll of Thunder, Hear My Cry

   Sample: I hoped to build my strength, to build my ability and reputation.

Using the Sentence-Composing Toolbox

2. To reassure herself, Emily reached inside her green velveteen coat, pulled out the gold locket that hung from a chain around her neck, and opened the clasp.

   Barbara Brooks Wallace, *Peppermints in the Parlor*

Sample: To impress him, John took out his battered old wallet, rifled through the different bills that were on hand inside the billfold, and chose a twenty.

3. It would be just to slay Gollum, this treacherous, murderous creature, and the only safe thing to do.

   J. R. R. Tolkien, *The Lord of the Rings*

Sample: It would be unforgivable to damage the china, that priceless, valuable heirloom, and the worst possible thing to destroy.

PRACTICE 5: EXPANDING

Below are sentences with the infinitive phrases omitted at the caret mark (^). For each caret, add an infinitive phrase, blending your content and style with the rest of the sentence.

1. ^ was wonderful, and a little terrifying.

   Arthur C. Clarke, *Dolphin Island*

2. Tim wanted ^ and ^, but he didn't dare move.

   Michael Crichton, *Jurassic Park*

3. He must be up early in the morning, ^, ^, and ^.

   Marjorie Kinnan Rawlings, *The Yearling*

CREATIVE WRITING

Revising a paragraph—To revise the plain paragraph below, at the caret marks (^) add infinitive phrases and other sentence-composing tools you've already learned.

"The Old House"

1. To ^, the kids approached the abandoned old house, ^.
2. On its front porch, ^, were rickety chairs and boxes and dusty empty bottles to ^.
3. The door, ^, was hanging off its hinges, ^.

Using the Sentence-Composing Toolbox

4. ^, they did not know if they should go inside to ^.

5. After discussing their fears, ^, they made a decision to ^.

6. To ^, they opened the dilapidated door and entered ^.

Write out your revision like a paragraph, not a list of sentences. Present your revised paragraph to your class to see the various effective ways you and your classmates revised the same plain paragraph to make it memorable.

Tip for Better Revising: Always, when you revise something you've written, look for places to use infinitive phrases and other sentence-composing tools to add detail, interest, and professional style to your writing.

Using the Sentence-Composing Toolbox

REVIEWING THE TOOLS: J. R. R. TOLKIEN'S *THE LORD OF THE RINGS*

Directions: Using these abbreviations, identify the underlined tools. If you need to review the tool, study the pages below.

Phrases	Review These Pages
absolute phrase = AB	pages 38–42
appositive phrase = AP	pages 44–48
prepositional phrase = PREP	pages 50–54
participial phrase (present or past) = P	pages 56–61
gerund phrase = G	pages 62–66
infinitive phrase = INF	pages 68–78

REVIEW 1: IDENTIFYING

Directions: Write the abbreviation of the underlined tool.

1. As the hideous Balrog fell, it swung its whip, and the thongs lashed and curled about Gandolf's knees, <u>dragging him to the brink of the pit</u>, where the wizard staggered, fell, and slid into the abyss.

2. <u>Down the face of a precipice</u>, sheer and almost smooth in the pale moonlight, the small black shape of Gollum was moving with his thin limbs splayed out.

3. Behind him came Gimli, <u>his eyes glinting in the dim light as he turned his head from side to side</u>.

4. The black horses, <u>filled with madness</u>, leapt forward in terror and bore their riders into the rushing flood.

5. After Sam unroped him, the Gollum got up and began <u>prancing about like a whipped dog whose master then petted it</u>.

6. There is a power in Rivendell <u>to resist the might of Mordo</u>, for a while.

7. This is the Master-ring, <u>the One Ring to rule them all</u>.

Using the Sentence-Composing Toolbox

Directions: Write the abbreviation of each underlined tool. Each sentence illustrates a combination of tools from the six tools listed above.

Example:

Sentence: (A) <u>Round the corner</u> came a black horse, (B) <u>no hobbit-pony but a full-sized horse</u>, and on it sat a large man, who seemed to crouch in the saddle, (C) <u>wrapped in a great black cloak and hood</u>, so that only his boots in the high stirrups showed below, (D) <u>his face shadowed and invisible</u>.

Answers:

(A)—PREP (prepositional)   (C)—P (past participle)

(B)—AP (appositive)   (D)—AB (absolute)

8. Frodo, even in that fair house, (A) <u>looking out upon a sunlit valley</u>, (B) <u>filled with the sound of clear waters</u>, felt a dread darkness in his heart.

9. (A) <u>To keep fear away until the very last</u>, Sam's eyes still strayed north, north into the eye of the wind, to where the sky far off was clear, as the cold blast, (B) <u>rising to a gale</u>, drove back the darkness.

10. There were five terrifying tall black figures, (A) <u>two standing on the lip of the dell</u>, (B) <u>three advancing</u>.

11. They saw nothing more, until they stumbled over the body of Frodo, (A) <u>lying as if dead</u>, (B) <u>face downwards on the grass</u> (C) <u>with his sword beneath him</u>.

12. As they came out again (A) <u>into the open country</u> (B) <u>at sundown</u>, they overtook an old man leaning on a staff, (C) <u>clothed in rags of grey or dirty white</u>.

13. Against the opposite wall was a long bench, (A) <u>filled with wide earthenware pottery</u>, and beside it stood a table with brown jugs of water, (B) <u>some cold</u>, (C) <u>some steaming hot</u>.

14. (A) <u>On the far side</u>, (B) <u>under the distant lamps</u>, they could just make out a dark figure, (C) <u>a menacing presence</u>, that swayed, then crawled back into the gloom beyond the lamps.

15. A huge orc, (A) <u>suited in black mail from head to foot</u>, leaped into the chaos, (B) <u>his eyes like coals</u>, (C) <u>his tongue red</u>, and (D) <u>diving with the speed of a striking snake</u>, he charged and thrust with his spear straight at Frodo.

Using the Sentence-Composing Toolbox

REVIEW 2: IMITATING

The model sentences below contain the six phrase tools you just reviewed—absolute, appositive, prepositional, participial, gerund, infinitive—as well as other kinds of sentence-composing tools. For each model sentence, write the letter of its imitation. Then write your own imitation of the same model.

Model Sentences:

1. At the Haven, after saying goodbye to Frodo, Sam stood far into the night, hearing only the sigh and murmur of the waves on the shore of Middle-earth, and the sound of them sank deep into his heart.

2. To prevent their getting separated and wandering in different directions, they went in single file, with Frodo leading.

3. The sun, a pale and watery yellow, was gleaming through the mist just above the west wall of the hollow in which they rested.

4. It was the sound of water that Merry heard, falling into his quiet sleep, water streaming down gently and then spreading, spreading irresistibly all round the house into a shoreless dark pool.

5. As injured Frodo clung upon Sam's back, arms loosely about his neck, legs clasped firmly under his arms, Sam staggered to his feet, but to his amazement the burden felt light.

Imitations:

A. It was the softness of velvet that Rachel felt, resting on her favorite pillow, velvet touching her softly and then warming, warming all over her face like the fur of a puppy.

B. To encourage their getting acquainted and socializing as a group, the new kids sat at one table, with no adults present.

C. While his stuffed bear hung from Aidan's hand, its head bobbing with Aidan's little body running, its face turned toward his, the little boy raced toward his daddy, and to his delight, the bear came, too.

D. Near the intersection, before crossing the street to Lancaster Avenue, Tiffany looked carefully in both directions, observing mainly the speed and directions of the cars on both lanes of the highway, and the volume of traffic made for a long wait.

E. The horse, a light and speckled thoroughbred, was grazing in the field right beside the barns of the track in which the horses ran.

Using the Sentence-Composing Toolbox

REVIEW 3: CREATING

The paragraph below is based upon an incident in *The Lord of the Rings:* Gollum steals the Ring from Frodo.

At the caret (^), use your imagination to add these phrases—absolute, appositive, prepositional, participial, gerund, infinitive—to make the paragraph good enough to appear in the original novel!

"The End of the Ring"

(1) Gollum, ^, darted out of the darkness toward Frodo to steal the Ring. (2) He grabbed for it on Frodo's finger, ^, but at his reptilian touch, Frodo struggled to prevent him, ^. (3) The two fought for the Ring, ^, at the edge of the fiery endless pit, the flames awakening and leaping up blazing red. (4) Frenzied, near the brink, Gollum, like a ferocious animal, bit Frodo's finger off, removed the Ring, thrust it onto his own finger held high and away from Frodo, and wailed, "My Precious! My Precious!" while blindly nearing the edge of the hellish pit, ^. (5) Dancing like a mad thing, ^, Gollum lost his balance and, with a shriek, fell down deeply into the burning abyss, ^, and the Ring was gone.

Add a few more spectacular sentences, with lots of sentence-composing tools!

Using the Sentence-Composing Toolbox

Sentence-Composing Tools: Clause Types

DEFINITION

Clauses are groups of words containing subjects and verbs. An independent clause can stand alone as a complete sentence. A dependent clause cannot stand alone because it is only a sentence part, not a complete sentence. Dependent clauses must be linked to independent clauses for their full meaning.

All sentences have at least one independent clause—frequently more—and many sentences also have dependent clauses.

There are three kinds of dependent clauses, taught later in this worktext: adjective clause (page 84), adverb clause (page 90), and noun clause (page 96). Both adjective clauses and adverb clauses are *outside* the independent clause to which they link; noun clauses are *inside* the independent clause to which they link.

Examples: Independent clauses are underlined, and dependent clauses are set in **boldface**.

1. **When flour was scarce**, the boy's mother would wrap the leftover biscuits in a clean flour sack and put them away for the next meal. *(The dependent clause—an adverb clause—is outside the independent clause.)*

    William H. Armstrong, *Sounder*

2. He pictured his father, **who must have been a shy and quiet boy, because he was a shy and quiet man**, seated with his group waiting to be called to the stage. *(The dependent clauses—an adjective clause and an adverb clause—are outside the independent clause.)*

    Lois Lowry, *The Giver*

3. Wilbur was **what farmers call a spring pig**. *(The dependent clause—a noun clause—is inside the independent clause.)*

    E. B. White, *Charlotte's Web*

Sentences with Only Independent Clauses:

1. About five o'clock the next morning the storm slammed into us with all its blizzardous fury. *(Contains one independent clause.)*

    Bill and Vera Cleaver, *Where the Lilies Bloom*

Using the Sentence-Composing Toolbox

2. <u>A frilly lace cap covered the woman's graying hair</u>, and <u>a long plain dress reached down to her ankles</u>. *(Contains two independent clauses joined by* and.*)*
   Larry Weinberg, *Ghost Hotel*

3. <u>A little corn was raised on the sterile slope</u>, and <u>it grew short and thick under the wind</u>, and <u>all the cobs formed on the landward sides of the stalks</u>. *(Contains three independent clauses joined by* and.*)*
   John Steinbeck, "Flight"

Sentences with Independent Clauses and Dependent Clauses:

4. <u>Catherine had loaded her oilcloth satchel with the leftovers from Sunday dinner, and we were enjoying a breakfast of cake and chicken</u> **when gunfire slapped through the woods**. *(Dependent clause is outside the independent clause.)*
   Truman Capote, *The Grass Harp*

5. <u>No one spoke at supper</u>, and <u>his mother</u>, **who sat next to him,** <u>leaned her head in her hand all through the meal, curving her fingers over her eyes so as not to see him</u>. *(Dependent clause is outside the independent clause.)*
   Gina Berriault, "The Stone Boy"

6. <u>I thought of</u> **how quickly dry timber becomes a roaring fire from a single spark**. *(Dependent clause is inside the independent clause.)*
   Eugenia Collier, "Sweet Potato Pie"

7. **Until I turned twelve years old,** <u>the kind of friends I had were</u> **what you'd expect**. *(The first dependent clause is outside the independent clause; the second is inside the independent clause.)*
   Joseph Krumgold, *Onion John*

PRACTICE 1: MATCHING

Match the dependent clauses with the sentences. Write out each sentence, inserting the dependent clauses at the caret (^) and underlining them.

Sentences:

1. A jury never looks at a defendant it has convicted, and ^, not one of them looked at Tom Robinson.
   Harper Lee, *To Kill a Mockingbird*

Dependent Clauses:

a. what I really couldn't imagine

Using the Sentence-Composing Toolbox

2. Ferdinand didn't look at ^, and instead of sitting on the nice, cool grass in the shade, he sat on a bumble bee.
   Munro Leaf, *The Story of Ferdinand*

3. His large face was fixed in a permanent expression of misery and despair, and his body, ^, had shrunk to the dimensions of a starving person.
   Paul Read Piers, *Alive*

4. ^ was Miss Love kissing him, much less marrying him.
   Olive Ann Burns, *Cold Sassy Tree*

5. That night he kept a fire going and sat watching for the lion, ^.
   Hal Borland, *When the Legends Die*

b. which had once been solid and strong

c. who came and prowled the nearby darkness, growling but fire-wary

d. where he was sitting

e. when this jury came in

PRACTICE 2: UNSCRAMBLING TO IMITATE

In the model and the scrambled list, identify the independent and dependent clauses. Next, unscramble and write out the sentence parts to imitate the model. Finally, write your own imitation of the model and identify the independent and dependent clauses.

MODEL: As Harry passed the window, he saw her deep in determined conversation with her friend Marietta, who was wearing a very thick layer of makeup, which did not entirely obscure the odd formation of pimples still etched across her face.
   J. K. Rowling, *Harry Potter and the Half-Blood Prince*

a. which was not quite keeping the frisky puppy

b. she noticed Mike caught in playful animation with their dog Skip

c. who was chewing a green toy bone of rubber

d. when Tiffany peeked into the room

e. with boundless energy always entertained by such an artificial treat

Using the Sentence-Composing Toolbox

PRACTICE 3: COMBINING TO IMITATE

In the model, identify the independent and dependent clauses. Next, combine the list of sentences to imitate the model. Finally, write your own imitation of the model and identify the independent and dependent clauses.

MODEL: The strange creature, which was still steaming and shaking itself, opened its mouth and began to make noises.

                    C. S. Lewis, *Out of the Silent Planet*

a. This sentence is about the lost child.

b. It was the child who was loudly crying and holding himself.

c. The child turned his head.

d. And the child started to see his parents.

PRACTICE 4: IMITATING

Identify the independent and dependent clauses in the models and sample imitations. Then choose one of the models and write an imitation of the entire sentence, one sentence part at a time. See if your classmates can guess your model.

Models:

1. The balmy summer air, the restful quiet, the odor of the flowers, and the drowsing murmur of the bees made Aunt Polly nod off over her knitting, for she had no company but the cat, and it was asleep in her lap. (Hint: *The first of the three independent clauses has four subjects and one verb.*)

                    Mark Twain, *The Adventures of Tom Sawyer*

Sample: The droning air conditioner, the quiet house, the lateness of the hour, and the pleasant sunset from his window made Grandfather remember other similar evenings, for he had no other entertainment but his memories, and they were movies in his mind.

2. With the ring of light from his lantern dancing from side to side, Mr. Jones lurched across the yard, kicked off his boots at the back door, drew himself a last glass of beer from the barrel, and made his way up to bed, where Mrs. Jones was already snoring. (Hint: *The independent clause has one subject with four verbs.*)

                    George Orwell, *Animal Farm*

Using the Sentence-Composing Toolbox

Sample: With the sound of cheering from his friends playing in his mind, Tom ran across the field, picked up the Frisbee in the ditch, gave himself an emphatic pat of congratulations on his back, and marched back across to the field, where the girls were loudly applauding.

3. When darkness had fallen over everything, and as the stars burned bright above them in the moonless sky, the children fell asleep. *(Hint: There are two dependent clauses.)*

   Cynthia Voigt, *Homecoming*

Sample: As order settled into the classroom, and while the students remained seated near them in the seventh-grade room, the administrators sat down.

PRACTICE 5: EXPANDING

Below are sentences with the clauses omitted at the caret mark (^). For each caret, add the indicated kind of clause (independent or dependent), blending your content and style with the rest of the sentence.

1. Because we sang every day and Mr. Rice was a gifted music teacher, ^. *(Add an independent clause.)*

   Katherine Paterson, *Jacob Have I Loved*

Note: It's okay to begin a sentence with *because* if you have an independent clause after it. This sentence has a dependent clause beginning with "because," and you're adding an independent clause, so everything's fine.

2. Frodo, hardly less terrified than his companions, was shivering, ^, but his terror was swallowed up in a sudden temptation to put on the Ring. *(Add a dependent clause.)*

   J. R. R. Tolkien, *The Lord of the Rings*

3. Driven by despair, ^, Taran groped for a handful of stones, of loose earth, even a broken twig to fling in defiance at the warrior, ^, blade upraised. *(Add two dependent clauses.)*

   Lloyd Alexander, *The High King*

Using the Sentence-Composing Toolbox

CREATIVE WRITING

Composing a paragraph—Pretend that you are one of the professional writers listed below who has written the first sentence of a long story. Use one of the sentences as the first sentence in a paragraph that will begin that story. Create the rest of the paragraph. Within your paragraph use independent and dependent clauses and other sentence-composing tools you've learned to make your paragraph memorable. In the starter sentences, independent clauses are underlined, and dependent clauses are set in **boldface**.

Reminder: Don't try to write a complete story. Write only the first paragraph of that story. (Maybe later you'll want to write the entire story!)

1. <u>The garden of paradise was a beautiful, beautiful place, with soft green grass shaded by trees</u>, **which bore blossoms and fruit at the same time, where sweet birds sang from morning to night**, and <u>all was innocence and peace</u>.
   Howard Pyle, *The Garden Behind the Moon*

2. <u>Crossing the lawn that summer morning, Douglas Spaulding broke a spider web with his face</u> **as a single invisible line on the air touched his brow and snapped without a sound.**
   Ray Bradbury, *Dandelion Wine*

3. <u>She heard something rustling on the matting</u>, and **when she looked down at the floor**, <u>she saw a snake gliding along and watching her with eyes like jewels</u>.
   Frances Hodgson Burnett, *The Secret Garden*

Using the Sentence-Composing Toolbox

Sentence-Composing Tools: Adjective Clause

DEFINITION

A dependent clause that describes a person, place, or thing. Like all clauses, adjective clauses contain a subject and its verb.

Adjective clauses are descriptive attachments to independent clauses and are, therefore, dependent clauses. They usually begin with one of these words: *who, which, whose*. They answer these questions:

What did the person, place, or thing do? *(who, which)*

What did the person, place, or thing have? *(whose)*

Who: The twins, **who had finished their homework**, were allowed to watch half an hour of TV.
                Madeleine L'Engle, *A Wrinkle in Time*

Which: The man on the loudspeaker begins calling everyone over to the track for the first event, **which is the 20-yard dash**.
                Toni Cade Bambara, "Raymond's Run"

Whose: Little Jon, **whose eyes were quicker than most**, should have seen the hole, but all his attention was on the stars.
                Alexander Key, *The Forgotten Door*

Two Positions for Adjective Clauses:

S-V split (between a subject and its verb): Miss Fleetie Breathitt, **who was the principal of our school as well as my teacher and sometimes Romey's**, said she was glad to see us again.
                Bill and Vera Cleaver, *Where the Lilies Bloom*

Closer (after a subject and its verb): The first thing they saw was Peeves the Poltergeist, **who was floating upside down in midair and stuffing the nearest keyhole with chewing gum**.
                J. K. Rowling, *Harry Potter and the Prisoner of Azkaban*

Using the Sentence-Composing Toolbox

Nonrestrictive vs. Restrictive Adjective Clauses:

Nonrestrictive (<u>Describes</u> a person, place, or thing, and is punctuated with commas): His black hair, **which had been combed wet earlier in the day**, was dry now and blowing.

                    J. D. Salinger, "The Laughing Man"

The nonrestrictive adjective clause doesn't identify the black hair; it describes it. Because there are pauses before and after "which had been combed wet earlier in the day," two commas are needed.

Restrictive (<u>Identifies</u> a person, place, or thing and is not punctuated with commas): Already we knew that there was one room in that region above stairs **which no one had seen in forty years**.

                    William Faulkner, "A Rose for Emily"

The restrictive adjective clause identifies the specific room. What room? The one "which no one had seen in forty years." Because there is no pause, a comma is not needed.

    In this section, only nonrestrictive adjective clauses are practiced as they are the kind that add descriptive detail to your writing.

Note: Adjective clauses are set in **boldface**, and independent clauses are <u>underlined</u>.

Single Adjective Clauses:

1. <u>Mr. McAlester</u>, **who kept the store**, <u>was a good Arkansas man</u>.
                    Charles Portis, *True Grit*

2. <u>The great coon dog</u>, **whose rhythmic panting came through the porch floor**, <u>came from under the house and began to whine</u>.
                    William H. Armstrong, *Sounder*

3. <u>He had a permanent case of sun itch</u>, **which he scratched continually without adding anything to his negligible beauty**.
                    Robert Heinlein, *The Green Hills of Earth*

Using the Sentence-Composing Toolbox

Multiple Adjective Clauses:

4. <u>In his room on the ground floor, Father Kleinsorge changed into a military uniform</u>, **which he had acquired when he was teaching at the Rokko Middle School in Kobe** and **which he wore during air-raid alerts**.

    John Hersey, *Hiroshima*

5. <u>She failed to see a shadow</u>, **which followed her like her own shadow**, **which stopped when she stopped**, and **which started again when she did**.

    Gaston Leroux, *The Phantom of the Opera*

6. <u>These are men of chemistry</u>, **who spray the trees against pests**, **who sulfur the grapes**, **who cut out diseases and rots, mildews and sicknesses**.

    John Steinbeck, *The Grapes of Wrath*

PRACTICE 1: MATCHING

Match the adjective clauses with the sentences. Write out each sentence, inserting the adjective clauses at the caret (^) and underlining them.

Sentences:

1. All the eyes of Paris were fixed on the Eiffel Tower, ^.

    Chris Van Allsburg, *The Sweetest Fig*

2. My hands were wrapped in an old towel, ^.

    Richard Kim, *Lost Names*

3. She also had to watch our three chickens, ^.

    Laurence Yep, *Dragonwings*

4. One guy, ^, tried to rise but could not.

    Charles Frazier, *Cold Mountain*

5. Behind her in the shadows, he could see the little boy, ^.

    Madeleine L'Engle, *A Wrinkle in Time*

Adjective Clauses:

a. which I also used to wipe the sweat from my face

b. whose wounds were so dreadful that he more resembled meat than man

c. who must have been about his own age

d. which slowly drooped over as if it were made of soft rubber

e. who loved to wander away from our farm

Using the Sentence-Composing Toolbox

PRACTICE 2: UNSCRAMBLING TO IMITATE

In the model and the scrambled list, identify the adjective clause. Next, unscramble and write out the sentence parts to imitate the model. Finally, write your own imitation of the model and identify the adjective clause.

MODEL: For several months, there had been nothing discussed at the Opera but this ghost in dress-clothes, who stalked about the building, from top to bottom, like a shadow, who spoke to nobody, and who vanished as soon as he was seen.
Gaston Leroux, *The Phantom of the Opera*

a. who believed no one

b. except the captain from the losing team

c. we had all forgotten about the scuffle

d. after a few days

e. from morning to night, like a robot

f. and who ranted as soon as he was challenged

g. who talked about the fight

PRACTICE 3: COMBINING TO IMITATE

In the model, identify the adjective clause. Next, combine the list of sentences to imitate the model. Finally, write your own imitation of the model and identify the adjective clause.

MODEL: Granny's uncle, who used to have a restaurant business feeding county prisoners, was in charge of Grandpa's cotton warehouse, one of the biggest in north Georgia, and also the store's cotton seed business.
Olive Ann Burns, *Cold Sassy Tree*

a. This sentence is about Maria's sister.

b. It was Maria who happened to be a big fan attending every game.

c. She was the head of the team's fan club.

d. That club was one of the biggest clubs in the school.

e. And Maria was also the head of the new uniform fund-raiser.

Using the Sentence-Composing Toolbox

PRACTICE 4: IMITATING

Identify the adjective clauses in the models and sample imitations. Then choose one of the models and write an imitation of the entire sentence, one sentence part at a time. See if your classmates can guess your model.

Models:

1. It seemed to Anne a terrible thing that she could not shed a tear for Matthew, who had been so kind to her, who had walked with her last evening at sunset, and who was now lying in a coffin in the dim room below with that awful peace on his brow.

   L. M. Montgomery, *Anne of Green Gables*

   Sample: It appeared to Tim a profound moment as he fulfilled his promise to his dad, who had always believed in him, who had spoken with Tim always about succeeding, and who was now sitting in the audience in the school's auditorium with a proud smile on his face.

2. Then they all climbed back up the wooden staircase, which creaked for five minutes under their heavy footsteps.

   Alexander Dumas, *The Count of Monte Cristo*

   Sample: Now the chorus performed so well at the school assembly, which echoed for an hour with their harmonious voices.

3. There was a gate in the wall, whose hinges were the bones of human feet and whose locks were jawbones set with sharp teeth.

   Post Wheeler, *Vasilissa the Beautiful*

   Sample: Inside stood the nanny for the child, whose giggles were the sound of wind chimes and whose appearance was a drawing from a children's book.

PRACTICE 5: EXPANDING

Below are sentences with the adjective clauses omitted at the caret mark (^). For each caret, add an adjective clause, blending your content and style with the rest of the sentence.

1. While Lottie disliked Miss Minchin, ^, and Miss Amelia, ^, she rather liked Sara.

   Frances Hodgson Burnett, *A Little Princess*

Using the Sentence-Composing Toolbox

2. She handed Turtle a peanut-butter cracker, ^, but it broke into smithereens.
   Barbara Kingsolver, *The Bean Trees*

3. He glanced at Snape, ^, and looked quickly away.
   J. K. Rowling, *Harry Potter and the Chamber of Secrets*

CREATIVE WRITING

Revising a paragraph—To revise the plain paragraph below, at the caret marks (^) add adjective clauses and other sentence-composing tools you've already learned.

"Extreme Recess"

1. The children, who ^, tumbled onto the playground, ^.
2. Their brightly colored clothing, which ^, looked like candy.
3. ^, some ran to the jungle gym, which ^.
4. Others, whose ^, started to play hopscotch, ^.
5. ^, a small group of girls, ^, played jump rope.
6. ^, the boys, who ^, stood together in a corner, ^.

Write out your revision like a paragraph, not a list of sentences. Present your revised paragraph to your class to see the various effective ways you and your classmates revised the same plain paragraph to make it memorable.

Tip for Better Revising: Always, when you revise something you've written, look for places to use adjective clauses and other sentence-composing tools to add detail, interest, and professional style to your writing.

Using the Sentence-Composing Toolbox

Sentence-Composing Tools: Adverb Clause

DEFINITION

A dependent clause that gives more information about the rest of the sentence. Like all clauses, adverb clauses contain a subject and its verb.

Adverb clauses answer these questions about an independent clause, and begin with the words (called *subordinate conjunctions*) in parentheses:

When does it happen? *(after, as, before, when, while, until)*

Why does it happen? *(because, since)*

How does it happen? *(as if)*

Under what condition does it happen? *(although, if)*

Example:

When he was nearly thirteen, my brother Jem got his arm badly broken at the elbow.
Harper Lee, To Kill a Mockingbird

Note: Sometimes students confuse adverb clauses with prepositional phrases. Both can begin with the same words. Here's how to tell the difference: If the first word is removed and what remains is a complete sentence, it is an adverb clause; however, if the first word is removed and a complete sentence does *not* result, it is a prepositional phrase.

Adverb clause: Mrs. Rachel, **before she had closed the door**, had taken mental note of everything that was on that table. First word *(before)* removed: **She had closed the door**. *(Complete sentence so it is an adverb clause.)*
L. M. Montgomery, Anne of Green Gables

Prepositional phrase: Mrs. Rachel, **before closing the door**, had taken mental note of everything that was on that table. First word *(before)* removed: **closing the door**. *(Not a complete sentence so it is a prepositional phrase, not an adverb clause.)*

Note: Adverb clauses are **set in boldface**, and independent clauses are <u>underlined</u>.

Single Adverb Clauses:

1. **While he scrubbed the sidewalk**, <u>I stood there throwing the ball at the apartment building that faced the street</u>.
Steve Allen, "The Sidewalk"

Using the Sentence-Composing Toolbox

2. <u>Lesley</u>, **when she felt the lawn mower bearing down on her,** <u>abandoned her half of the wide handle and leaped out of the way</u>.
   Lynne Reid Banks, One More River

3. <u>Dicey was up and dressed, washed and fed, and out the door, with the day's work outlined in her head</u>, **before anyone else stirred in the silent house**.
   Cynthia Voigt, Seventeen Against the Dealer

Multiple Adverb Clauses:

4. <u>With a gentle forefinger, he stroked the turtle's throat and chest</u> **until the horny-toad relaxed, until its eyes closed and it lay languorous and asleep**.
   John Steinbeck, The Red Pony

5. <u>One fall</u>, **before he had regained his full strength**, <u>a young woman came to teach in the island school</u>, and <u>somehow</u>, **although I was never able to understand it fully**, <u>the elegant little schoolmistress fell in love with my large, red-faced, game-legged father</u>, and <u>they were married</u>. *(Contains three independent clauses connected by and.)*
   Katherine Paterson, Jacob Have I Loved

6. <u>They waited until night</u> because nobody could see them at night, because Atticus would be so deep in a book he wouldn't hear the Kingdom coming, because if Boo Radley killed them they'd miss school instead of vacation, and because it was easier to see inside a dark house in the dark than in the daytime.
   Harper Lee, To Kill a Mockingbird

PRACTICE 1: MATCHING

Match the adverb clauses with the sentences. Write out each sentence, inserting the adverb clauses at the caret (^) and underlining them.

Sentences:

1. ^, that activity will turn him into a good boy.
   Louis Sachar, Holes

Adverb Clauses:

a. as she stepped into the light

Using the Sentence-Composing Toolbox

2. Her face, ^, was round and thick, and her eyes were like two immense eggs stuck into a white mess of bread dough.
   Ray Bradbury, *The Martian Chronicles*

3. ^, their grandmother was waiting in the kitchen.
   Cynthia Voigt, *Homecoming*

4. ^, the gods will grant her wish and make her healthy.
   Eleanor Coerr, *Sadako and the Thousand Paper Cranes*

5. The first floor, ^, was where the rats lived.
   Walter Dean Myers, *Motown and Didi*

b. because it was closest to the garbage in the empty lot

c. if a sick person folds one thousand paper cranes

d. if you make a bad boy dig a hole every day in the hot sun

e. when the children came downstairs for breakfast

PRACTICE 2: UNSCRAMBLING TO IMITATE

In the model and the scrambled list, identify the adverb clause. Next, unscramble and write out the sentence parts to imitate the model. Finally, write your own imitation of the model and identify the adverb clause.

MODEL: After Mrs. Mallard had laid eight eggs in the nest, she couldn't go to visit Michael any more, because she had to sit on the eggs to keep them warm.
   Robert McCloskey, *Make Way for Ducklings*

a. to figure things out

b. he couldn't begin to understand his camera very much

c. before Uncle Al had studied digital photography in school

d. since he had to puzzle over the manual

PRACTICE 3: COMBINING TO IMITATE

In the model, identify the adverb clause. Next, combine the list of sentences to imitate the model. Finally, write your own imitation of the model and identify the adverb clause.

Using the Sentence-Composing Toolbox

MODEL: The truck drivers, when they heard that Maxie Hammerman had been released, were furious.

                            Jean Merrill, *The Pushcart War*

a. This sentence is about the ninth graders.

b. It's about the time when they saw that the high school had been air-conditioned.

c. When they saw that that had happened they were thrilled.

PRACTICE 4: IMITATING

Identify the adverb clauses in the models and sample imitations. Then choose one of the models and write an imitation of the entire sentence, one sentence part at a time. See if your classmates can guess your model.

Models:

1. Fred Snood, the superintendent, checked the cellar storage cages, after a passing youth hinted to him that there had been a robbery.

                            Emily Neville, *It's Like This, Cat*

Sample: Alma Brown, the teacher, missed the three absent students, although the other children communicated to her that they had not noticed their absences.

2. On the Titanic, the porthole in his cabin was open, and as the iceberg brushed by, chunks of ice fell into the cabin.

                            Walter Lord, *A Night to Remember*

Sample: In the morning, the sunshine in the yard was strong, and as the sun rose higher, rays of light spread over the porch.

3. When he was in school, he longed to be out, and when he was out, he longed to be in.

                            Norton Juster, *The Phantom Tollbooth*

Sample: When she was a child, she wanted to be an adult, but after she became an adult, she wanted to be a child.

Using the Sentence-Composing Toolbox

PRACTICE 5: EXPANDING

Below are sentences with the adverb clauses omitted at the caret mark (^). For each caret, add an adverb clause, blending your content and style with the rest of the sentence.

1. The horse was a magnificent black creature with long legs, brown eyes, and a splendid flowing mane, and **because** ^, he got along well with the fairies, who lived in a nearby hill, and with the humans, who lived in a nearby hamlet and earned a living by farming and fishing.
   Winifred Finlay, "The Water-Horse of Barra"

2. I was just fourteen years of age **when** ^.
   Charles Portis, *True Grit*

3. The pupils of his eyes grew smaller and smaller, **as though** ^, **until** ^, **until** ^.
   Madeleine L'Engle, *A Wrinkle in Time*

CREATIVE WRITING

Composing a paragraph—Pretend that you are one of the professional writers listed below who has written the first sentence of a long story. Use one of the sentences as the first sentence in a paragraph that will begin that story. Create the rest of the paragraph. Just as the writers' sentences use adverb clauses, within your paragraph use adverb clauses and other sentence-composing tools you've learned to make your paragraph memorable.

Reminder: Don't try to write a complete story. Write only the first paragraph of that story! (Maybe later you'll want to write the entire story!)

1. **When I was in elementary school**, I packed my suitcase and told my mother I was going to run away.
   Jean Craighead George, *My Side of the Mountain*

2. **Though it was blind**, I couldn't kill it, and yet I knew it would have a hard time to live.
   Jesse Stuart, "Thanksgiving Hunter"

Using the Sentence-Composing Toolbox

3. Shrinking is always more painful than growing, **since for a moment all your bones jam together like a crowd on market day**, but the pain was over quickly enough **as I became the size of a cat**.

   Laurence Yep, *Dragon of the Lost Sea*

Using the Sentence-Composing Toolbox

Sentence-Composing Tools: Noun Clause

DEFINITION

A dependent clause that works like a noun. Like all clauses, noun clauses contain a subject and its verb.

To see how noun clauses act like nouns, insert *what we eat for breakfast* into any of these blanks:

1. ____ is important. *(subject)*

2. We discussed ____. *(direct object)*

3. The health teacher talked about ____. *(object of preposition)*

4. A valuable part of a healthy diet is ____. *(predicate noun)*

5. A regular morning meal, ____, provides energy for school. *(appositive)*

Most noun clauses begin with *that, what,* or *how.* However, some noun clauses begin with other words. The best way to identify a noun clause is this: If a clause is removable, it's not a noun clause; if a clause is *not* removable, it is a noun clause.

Removable (adverb or adjective clauses):

1. The exact year **when George Washington was born** was 1732. *(adjective clause)*

2. **When George Washington was born**, cars didn't exist. *(adverb clause)*

Not Removable (noun clauses):

3. **When George Washington was born** was a question on the quiz.

4. The discussion was about **when George Washington was born**.

5. Mr. Jameson discussed **when George Washington was born**.

Single Noun Clauses:

1. Lucy stepped into the wardrobe and got in among the fur coats and rubbed her face against them, leaving the door open, of course, because she knew **that it is very foolish to shut oneself into any wardrobe**.

     C. S. Lewis, *The Chronicles of Narnia*

Using the Sentence-Composing Toolbox

2. He wondered **what she wanted**.

    Gaston Leroux, *The Phantom of the Opera*

3. Aunt Pearl was the last one out, telling the Reverend **how much she enjoyed his sermon**.

    Robert Lipsyte, *The Contender*

Multiple Noun Clauses:

4. The first moment I saw you I knew **that you wanted a bicycle, that getting one was very important to you**, and **that you meant to earn the money for one this summer if you could**.

    Stephen King, *Hearts in Atlantis*

5. **What each man contributes to the sum of knowledge** is **what counts**.

    Daniel Keyes, *Flowers for Algernon*

6. It doesn't matter **how you write the first draft or even the second draft**, but it makes all the difference in the world **how you write the final draft**.

    Elizabeth White *(saying)*

PRACTICE 1: MATCHING

Match the noun clauses with the sentences. Write out each sentence, inserting the noun clauses at the caret (^) and underlining the noun clauses.

Sentences:

1. Aunt Petunia often said that Dudley looked like an angel; Harry often said ^.

    J. K. Rowling, *Harry Potter and the Sorcerer's Stone*

2. He crept carefully, until no one who might be watching could tell ^.

    Robert Lipsyte, *The Contender*

3. He practiced on the sawhorse ^.

    John Steinbeck, *The Red Pony*

Noun Clauses:

a. how he would hold the reins in his left hand and a hat in his right hand

b. what I am

c. what attracted Mrs. Frisby's attention the most

Using the Sentence-Composing Toolbox

4. ^ was a box in one corner of the room, a box with dials and a small light shining on the front.
   Robert C. O'Brien, Mrs. Frisby and the Rats of NIMH

5. EPILEPSY: It's what I have, not ^.
   Slogan of Epilepsy Society of America

d. that Dudley looked like a pig in a wig

e. where he had come from

PRACTICE 2: UNSCRAMBLING TO IMITATE

In the model and the scrambled list, identify the noun clause. Next, unscramble and write out the sentence parts to imitate the model. Finally, write your own imitation of the model and identify the noun clause.

MODEL: Harry was unsurprised to see that the two best friends were whispering together, looking distressed.
J. K. Rowling, Harry Potter and the Half-Blood Prince

a. to hear

b. giggling together

c. Levon was interested

d. what the small children were talking about

PRACTICE 3: COMBINING TO IMITATE

In the model, identify the noun clause. Next, combine the list of sentences to imitate the model. Finally, write your own imitation of the model and identify the noun clause.

MODEL: Frodo thought that he heard a faint hiss and smelled venomous breath and felt a piercing chill.
J. R. R. Tolkien, The Lord of the Rings

a. This sentence is about Jeremiah.

b. Jeremiah felt something.

c. He felt that he gave a small contribution.

d. And he felt that he made some slight difference.

e. And he felt that he took a forward step.

Using the Sentence-Composing Toolbox

PRACTICE 4: IMITATING

Identify the noun clauses in the models and sample imitations. Then choose one of the models and write an imitation of the entire sentence, one sentence part at a time. See if your classmates can guess your model.

Models:

1. It could have been a trick, what Jim Thatcher said about the man.

    Hal Borland, *When the Legends Die*

    Sample: It might have been an excuse, how Willie Cranston got out of trouble.

2. Very late, a policeman stopped to see what they were up to.

    Frank Bonham, *Chief*

    Sample: Quite unexpectedly, a letter arrived to announce what they had won earlier.

3. As he was lifted to his feet, he knew that the dinosaur had his head in its jaws, and the horror of that realization was followed by a final wish, that it would all be ended soon.

    Michael Crichton, *Jurassic Park*

    Sample: While she was busy with her cooking, she wondered what the children were up to in the basement, and that nagging question in her mind was responsible for a quick detour, what a mother does many times each day.

PRACTICE 5: EXPANDING

Below are sentences with the noun clauses omitted at the caret mark (^). For each caret, add a noun clause, blending your content and style with the rest of the sentence.

1. About midnight, huddled and shivering under his blankets in the darkness, he began to wonder ^.

    Thomas Rockwell, *How to Eat Fried Worms*

2. As she headed down the hall to her next class, Geraldine remembered ^.

    Toni Cade Bambara, "Geraldine Moore the Poet"

3. Harry knew ^, ^, and ^.

    J. K. Rowling, *Harry Potter and the Half-Blood Prince*

Using the Sentence-Composing Toolbox

CREATIVE WRITING

Revising a paragraph—To revise the plain paragraph below, at the caret marks (^) add noun clauses and other sentence-composing tool you've already learned.

"Top Secret"

1. She walked into the auditorium, not knowing that ^.
2. ^, she had thought that ^.
3. All around her were other students who knew that ^.
4. She felt very much abandoned, ^, until her best friend arrived and told her what ^.
5. Then she understood what ^.
6. ^, she no longer wanted to know how or why ^.

Write out your revision like a paragraph, not a list of sentences. Present your revised paragraph to your class to see the various effective ways you and your classmates revised the same plain paragraph to make it memorable.

Tip for Better Revising: Always, when you revise something you've written, look for places to use noun clauses and other sentence-composing tools to add detail, interest, and professional style to your writing.

Using the Sentence-Composing Toolbox

REVIEWING THE TOOLS: C. S. LEWIS' *THE CHRONICLES OF NARNIA*

Directions: Using these abbreviations, identify the underlined tools. If you need to review the tool, study the pages below.

Clauses	Review These Pages
independent clause = INDC	pages 78–83
adjective clause = ADJC	pages 84–89
adverb clause = ADVC	pages 90–95
noun clause = NC	pages 96–100

REVIEW 1: IDENTIFYING

Directions: Write the abbreviation of the underlined tool.

1. People who have not been in Narnia sometimes think <u>that a thing cannot be good and terrible at the same time</u>.

2. Next moment, Lucy got rather a fright, for <u>she found herself caught up in mid-air between the Giant's finger and thumb</u>.

3. Reepicheep the Mouse, <u>who never felt that the ship was getting on fast enough</u>, loved to sit on the bulwark just behind the dragon's head, gazing out at the horizon and singing softly in his little chirping voice.

4. He had turned into a dragon <u>while he was asleep</u>.

5. Sleeping on a dragon's hoard, with greedy dragonish thoughts in his heart, <u>he had turned into a dragon himself</u>.

6. The bracelet, <u>which had fitted very nicely on the upper arm of Eustace the boy</u>, was far too small for the thick, stumpy foreleg of Eustace the dragon.

7. Lucy, sitting close to Aslan and divinely comfortable, wondered <u>what the trees were doing</u>.

8. <u>When they tried to look at Aslan's face</u>, they just caught a glimpse of the golden mane and the great, royal, solemn, overwhelming eyes.

Using the Sentence-Composing Toolbox

Directions: Write the abbreviation of each underlined tool. Each sentence contains a combination of tools from the four tools listed above.

Example:

Sentence: The best thing of all about the feast was (A) <u>that there was no breaking up or going away</u>, but (B) <u>as the talk grew quieter and slower</u>, (C) <u>the Narnians, one after the other, would begin to nod and finally drop off to sleep with feet towards the fire and good friends on either side</u>, (D) <u>whose conversation finally turned to sleepy silence all around the circle</u>.

Answers:

(A)—NC (noun clause)   (C)—INDC (independent clause)

(B)—ADVC (adverb clause)   (D)—ADJC (adjective clause)

9. (A) <u>There was a boy called Eustace Clarence Scrubb</u>, and (B) <u>he almost deserved that horrible name</u>.

10. (A) <u>Eustace Clarence liked animals, especially beetles</u>, (B) <u>if they were dead and pinned on a card</u>.

11. (A) <u>The quarreling giants stormed and jeered at one another, foamed and gibbered and jumped in their rage</u>, and (B) <u>each jump shook the earth like a bomb</u>.

12. Through the door of the Great Hall, (A) <u>which was wide open</u>, (B) <u>came the voices of the mermen and the mermaids</u>, swimming close to the shore and singing in honor of their new Kings and Queens.

13. (A) <u>Peter was tugging and pulling</u>, and (B) <u>the Wolf seemed neither alive nor dead</u>, and (C) <u>its bared teeth knocked against his forehead</u>, and (D) <u>everything was blood and heat and hair</u>.

14. (A) <u>The next moment they all came tumbling out of a wardrobe door into the empty room</u>, and (B) <u>they were no longer Kings and Queens in their regal hunting array but just Peter, Susan, Edmund, and Lucy in their old clothes</u>.

15. (A) <u>All their life in this world and all their adventures in Narnia had only been the cover and the title page</u>, (B) <u>because now at last they were beginning Chapter One of the Great Story</u>, (C) <u>which no one on earth has read</u>, (D) <u>which goes on forever</u>, (E) <u>which is a story in which every chapter is better than the one before</u>.

Using the Sentence-Composing Toolbox

REVIEW 2: IMITATING

The model sentences below contain the four tools you just reviewed—independent clauses, adjective clauses, adverb clauses, and noun clauses—as well as other kinds of sentence-composing tools. For each model sentence, write the letter of its imitation. Then write your own imitation of the same model.

Model Sentences:

1. With repeated blows, the Prince hacked off the serpent's head, but the horrible thing went on moving and coiling like a nasty bit of wire.

2. What hung over everyone like a cloud was the problem of what to do with their dragon when they were ready to sail.

3. Another roar of mean laughter went up from the Witch's followers as an ogre with a pair of shears came forward and squatted down by Aslan's head to cut the lion's mane.

4. In the last days of Narnia, there lived an Ape, clever, ugly, and wrinkled, and so old that no one could remember when he had first come to live in those parts.

5. As they came to the edge of the woods, there on the sand, like a giant lizard, or a flexible crocodile, or a serpent with legs, huge and horrible and humpy, crouched the dragon.

Imitations:

A. At the end of Gina's day, there came a sleep, welcome, soothing, and blissful, and so restful that she could not recall when she had gone to sleep in such comfort.

B. More children with fantastic costumes came out from the dark entrance as a costumed Cinderella with a basket full of treats appeared and turned on the overhead light to see the children's costumes.

C. What annoyed the passengers like nasty mosquitoes were the jokes about what horrible things would happen to them all as the plane was attempting to land.

D. When they stopped at the top of the Ferris wheel, there on the ground below, like a toy town, or a midget's playground, or a doll's village with colored lights, miniature and magical and wonderful, were the circus grounds.

E. With a calm smile, the cashier ignored the child's outburst, but the disappointed kid kept on whimpering and wailing like a spoiled brat in total tantrum.

Using the Sentence-Composing Toolbox

REVIEW 3: CREATING

The paragraph below is based upon an incident in *The Chronicles of Narnia*: The supernatural lion named Aslan gives two young girls, Lucy and Susan, a wonderful ride on his back through the sky.

At the caret (^), use your imagination to add independent clauses, adjective clauses, adverb clauses, and noun clauses to make the paragraph good enough to appear in the original novel!

"The Mystical Ride on the Lion's Back"

(1) After Aslan the lion suddenly, quite miraculously came back to life following his cruel death at the hands of the Witch, the animal gave Lucy and Susan a ride on his golden velvety back, a fantastic ride gliding fast and silent through the woods, and when ^, the little girls shouted joyously from the wonder of their ride. (2) His mane flying back in the wind, the lion ^. (3) Going twice as fast as the fastest horse, Aslan never seemed to grow tired because ^. (4) Zooming through the forest, which ^, threading the paths between tree trunks, jumping over bushes and smaller streams, Aslan transported the children, who fantasized that ^. (5) Aslan and the little passengers astride his back, who ^, soared up the hill, past the roaring waterfall, and then darted across the mountain toward the blazing sunset.

> **Add a few more spectacular sentences, with lots of sentence-composing tools!**

Creating Good Writing

From your sentence-composing toolbox filled with all the tools you've learned, get out your power tools to put them to work.

In this final section of *Grammar for Middle School: A Sentence-Composing Approach*, you'll partner with J. K. Rowling, author of the Harry Potter novels, to add sentence-composing tools you've learned in this worktext to an original paragraph titled "Harry and the Horrible Heffle." Then you'll write an original episode for the Harry Potter story with your own sentences built much like the sentences of J. K. Rowling. *Note:* Your teacher will tell you which tools from this list to use for the two creative writing assignments.

The Sentence-Composing Power Tools

(To review any of the tools, study the pages in parentheses.)

Words:

1. *Opening adjective (pages 12–16):* **Furious**, Harry threw his ingredients and his bag into his cauldron and dragged it up to the front of the dungeon to the empty table.
    Harry Potter and the Goblet of Fire

2. *Delayed adjective (pages 18–22):* Harry was on his feet again, **furious, ready to fly at Dumbledore**, who had plainly not understood Sirius at all.
    Harry Potter and the Order of the Phoenix

3. *Opening adverb (pages 24–28):* **Slowly, very slowly**, the snake raised its head until its eyes were on a level with Harry's.
    Harry Potter and the Sorcerer's Stone

4. *Delayed adverb (pages 30–37):* The gigantic snake was nearing Frank, and then, **incredibly, miraculously**, it passed him, following the spitting, hissing noises made by the cold voice beyond the door.
    Harry Potter and the Goblet of Fire

Phrases:

5. *Absolute (pages 38–42):* Soon, the crowd of gnomes in the field started walking away in a staggering line, **their little shoulders hunched**.
    Harry Potter and the Chamber of Secrets

Creating Good Writing

6. *Appositive (pages 44–48):* Fudge, **a portly little man in a long, pinstriped cloak**, looked cold and exhausted.
   Harry Potter and the Prisoner of Azkaban

7. *Preposition (pages 50–54):* **At daybreak on a fine summer's morning**, when the Riddle House had still been well kept and impressive, a maid had entered the drawing room to find all three Riddles dead.
   Harry Potter and the Chamber of Secrets

8. *Participial (pages 56–61):* **Hating himself, repulsed by what he was doing**, Harry forced the goblet back toward Dumbledore's mouth and tipped it for Dumbledore to drink the remainder of the horrible potion inside. *(Note: Contains both present and past participial phrases.)*
   Harry Potter and the Half-Blood Prince

9. *Gerund (pages 62–66):* **Conjuring up portable, waterproof fires** was a specialty of Hermione's.
   Harry Potter and the Chamber of Secrets

10. *Infinitive (pages 68–72):* **To make Dudley feel better about eating "rabbit food,"** Aunt Petunia had insisted that the whole family follow the same diet, too.
    Harry Potter and the Goblet of Fire

Clauses:

11. *Independent clause (pages 78–83):* **He raised the wand above his head and brought it swishing down through the dusty air** as a stream of red and gold sparks shot from the end like a firework, throwing dancing spots of light onto the walls. *(See also sentence 13 below.)*
    Harry Potter and the Sorcerer's Stone

12. *Adjective clause (pages 84–89):* The first thing they saw was Peeves the Poltergeist, **who was floating upside down in midair and stuffing the nearest keyhole with chewing gum**.
    Harry Potter and the Prisoner of Azkaban

Creating Good Writing

13. *Adverb clause (pages 90–95):* He raised the wand above his head and brought it swishing down through the dusty air **as a stream of red and gold sparks shot from the end like a firework, throwing dancing spots of light onto the walls.** *(See also sentence 11 above.)*
    Harry Potter and the Sorcerer's Stone

14. *Noun clause (pages 96–100):* Harry knew **that Dumbledore was going to refuse, that he would tell Riddle there would be plenty of time for practical demonstrations at Hogwarts, and that they were currently in a building full of Muggles and must therefore be cautious.**
    Harry Potter and the Half-Blood Prince

To boost the power of your tools, include the kinds of variety that good writers like J. K. Rowling use:

Length: Make some tools short (two to five words), some medium (six to ten words), some long (eleven or more words).

Position: For tools that can occur in more than one place in a sentence, use a variety of positions: openers, s-v splits, closers.

Number: Include within the same sentence two or more of the same tool: two or more appositives, two or more adverb clauses, two or more participles, and so on to create sentences with multiples.

Combination: Mix within the same sentence two or more different kinds of tools to create sentences with combinations.

In these final creative writing activities of *Grammar for Middle School: A Sentence-Composing Approach*, use all your power tools in all varieties to build memorable writing so good it could be published in a Harry Potter novel.

Creating Good Writing

CREATIVE WRITING

Revising a paragraph—To revise the plain paragraph below, at the caret marks (^) add a variety of sentence-composing tools you've already learned. Use your imagination to conjure up powerful sentence-composing tools to insert into the sentences. Make the paragraph much more exciting and memorable, like paragraphs from the real Harry Potter story. *Note:* Your teacher will tell you which tools to use from the list of pages 105–107.

"Harry and the Horrible Heffle"

(1) Down the stairs came a heffle, ^. (2) ^, Harry had only seen a heffle once before, when he and Ron, ^, were in the remotest recesses of the Hogwarts dungeon, ^. (3) ^, he remembered the horrifying sound a heffle makes, ^. (4) In Charms class, Professor Flitwick had taught them one spell that could disable a heffle, ^, and now Harry was trying desperately to remember it. (5) At moments like this, Harry missed Hermione, ^, and Ron, ^. (6) Now the heffle was halfway down the stairs, glaring at Harry, ^. (7) ^, the heffle started making that awful sound, ^, and Harry knew his time was running out. (8) A magic sword, ^, was locked in the glass bookcase a few feet away from Harry, ^.

Add a few more spectacular sentences, with lots of sentence-composing tools!

CREATIVE WRITING

Creating an episode—Pretend you are author J. K. Rowling and your publisher wants you to write a new episode of several paragraphs for Harry Potter about a new character for the series: either Harry's long-lost sister, Harriet Potter, or his long-lost brother, Philip Potter.

Because you are inventing a brand-new character—Harry's sister, Harriet, or brother, Philip—it may help to learn how J. K. Rowling invented Harry:

> The funny thing is that Harry came into my head almost completely formed. I saw him very, very clearly. I could see this skinny little boy with black hair, this weird scar on his forehead. I knew instantly that he was a wizard, but he didn't know that yet. Then I began to work out his background. That was the basic idea. He's a boy who is magic but doesn't yet know. So I'm thinking, well how can he not know. You know, so I worked backwards from that point. It was

Creating Good Writing

almost like the story was already there waiting for me to find it and it seemed to me the most watertight explanation for him not knowing that he was a wizard was that his parents had been a witch and wizard who had died and that he had been raised by Muggles, non-magic people. (from a radio interview with J. K. Rowling in 1999 by Christopher Lydon)

Using J. K. Rowling's writing style, write your episode about an exciting incident featuring Harriet or Philip Potter, done so well that your readers will think it was written by J. K. Rowling. *Note:* Your teacher will tell you which tools to use for your episode from the list on pages 105–107.

Use this Checklist to Plan and Write Your Episode:

- ☑ Jot down ideas you want to include in your episode. *(prewriting)*
- ☑ Write a draft of your episode. *(drafting)*
- ☑ Include the sentence-composing tools your teacher selected from the list on pages 105–107. *(drafting)*
- ☑ Show your draft to students in your class for suggestions. *(peer response)*
- ☑ Follow good suggestions from peers to revise your episode. *(revising)*
- ☑ Correct misspellings and errors in grammar and punctuation. *(editing)*
- ☑ Prepare a neat and attractive final copy for others to read, including your teacher. *(publishing)*

Asked her advice for young people who want to write, J. K. Rowling said, "The most important thing is to read as much as you can, like I did. It will give you an understanding of what makes good writing, and it will enlarge your vocabulary. And it's a lot of fun!"

Smart advice. As you continue to develop as a writer, read often and pay attention to good sentences. Write lots of them. Have fun.

> When it comes to language, nothing is more satisfying than to write a good sentence.
> —Barbara Tuchman

More help for middle school writers from the Killgallons

Sentence Composing for Middle School

A Worktext on Sentence Variety and Maturity
Don Killgallon

In **Sentence Composing for Middle School**, Don Killgallon presents a worktext based on a proven methodology that supports increasing maturity in middle school writers.

Unlike traditional grammar books that emphasize parsing, Killgallon asks students to imitate professional writers. He makes sentence composition enjoyable and challenging, teaching students to intuit their way to better writing.

Sentence Composing for Middle School produces sentence maturity and variety through practice in four sentence-manipulating techniques: sentence unscrambling, sentence imitating, sentence combining, and sentence expanding—all based on model sentences written by popular and widely respected authors.

Sentence Composing works in any middle school, with any student. Let it work with yours.

1997 / 144pp / $20.00
978-0-86709-419-0 / 0-86709-419-2

www.heinemann.com

To place an order, **call 800.225.5800**, or fax 877.231.6980